CITYSPOTS
BRATISLAVA

Thomas Cook

WHAT'S IN YOUR GUIDEBOOK?

Independent authors Impartial up-to-date information from our travel experts who meticulously source local knowledge.

Experience Thomas Cook's 165 years in the travel industry and guidebook publishing enriches every word with expertise you can trust.

Travel know-how Contributions by thousands of staff around the globe, each one living and breathing travel.

Editors Travel-publishing professionals, pulling everything together to craft a perfect blend of words, pictures, maps and design.

You, the traveller We deliver a practical, no-nonsense approach to information, geared to how you really use it.

CITYSPOTS
BRATISLAVA

Wendy Wrangham

Written by Wendy Wrangham
Original photography by Wendy Wrangham
Front cover photography (St Michael's Gate and Tower © Wilfried Krecichwost/
Getty Images
Series design based on an original concept by Studio 183 Limited

Produced by Cambridge Publishing Management Limited
Project Editor: Ross Hilton
Layout: Trevor Double
Maps: PC Graphics
Transport map: © Communicarta Limited

Published by Thomas Cook Publishing
A division of Thomas Cook Tour Operations Limited
Company Registration No. 1450464 England
PO Box 227, Unit 18, Coningsby Road
Peterborough PE3 8SB, United Kingdom
email: books@thomascook.com
www.thomascookpublishing.com
+ 44 (0) 1733 416477
ISBN: 978-1-84157-616-9

First edition © 2007 Thomas Cook Publishing
Text © 2007 Thomas Cook Publishing
Maps © 2007 Thomas Cook Publishing
Series/Project Editor: Kelly Anne Pipes
Production/DTP: Steven Collins

Printed and bound in Spain by GraphyCems

CONTENTS

SYMBOLS KEY

The following symbols are used throughout this book:

ⓐ address   ☎ telephone   ⓦ website address

🕑 opening times   Ⓝ public transport connections   ❶ important

---

The following symbols are used on the maps:

𝒊 information office	O city
✈ airport	O large town
➕ hospital	○ small town
Ⓩ police station	═ motorway
🚌 bus station	─ main road
🚆 railway station	─ minor road
✝ cathedral	─ railway
❶ numbers denote featured cafés & restaurants	

Hotels and restaurants are graded by approximate price as follows:

£ budget   ££ mid-range   £££ expensive

◐ *Bratislavsý hrad (Bratislava Castle) seen from the Old Town Hall tower*

INTRODUCING
Bratislava

Introduction

It is an acknowledged truth that Slovaks have a world-beating ice hockey team, but put them on the rink with the Czech Republic and they tend to lose. However, there are many changes and developments afoot in Bratislava and they all point to one thing: Bratislava, the little big city, is no longer playing second fiddle to Prague.

For centuries Bratislava held a key position sitting in the centre of Europe and on the River Danube. It has held numerous names (including Wratisslaburgium and Istropolis), been ruled by the Hungarians, unsuccessfully besieged by the Turks, hardly beautified by the communists and today it is being explored by everyone.

Bratislava lies on the border with Hungary and Austria thus producing two claims to fame: it is the only capital bordering two nations; and it and Vienna are the two closest capital cities in the world. The Small Carpathian Mountains dwindle into the city and give rise to excellent wine country and rural pursuits in the suburbs.

Culturally, Bratislava has hosted Mozart and Liszt. The National Theatre and Philharmonic Orchestra attract audiences for superlative performances and value for money. Galleries, museums and castles abound, laying testament to its long and varied cultural and historical past. And yet, Bratislava has a decidedly modern atmosphere with a social scene that meanders wildly between turn-of-the-century cafés, sleek chic restaurants and clubs in nuclear bunkers.

The mélange is fairly neatly contained in an area that can be easily walked, although trams and trolley buses ply their trade to distant sights and sounds. The twists and turns of cobbled streets can and invariably do lead to another discovery or even just a seat to sit and watch the world go by.

The vineyards, castles, ski slopes, spas and beautiful countryside will tempt you to stay longer, but if your stay is limited in length, you will still discover a city steeped in history, littered with palaces and pulsing to a vibrant beat.

⬤ Art is a common feature of Bratislava's streets

When to go

SEASONS & CLIMATE

Situated as it is in Central Europe with little elevation, Bratislava's climate is continental with warm, often hot, summers punctuated by sharp thunderstorms. The cold winters usually produce snowfalls with the coldest temperatures occurring around January. Bratislava does have four seasons, although spring and autumn can be nonexistent as daily temperatures tend to fluctuate from 22°C (72°F) to around freezing in one day at the turn of the seasons.

The High Tatras Mountains to the north gratefully receive copious snowfall for the resorts but this has also caused avalanches. The unpredictability of the mountain weather is mirrored to a lesser degree in Bratislava so a hat, sunscreen, sweater and umbrella are all useful day pack items.

Bratislavans head out of the city most weekends to their *chata* (holiday home). As ever, summer has many more tourists than winter. September and October see national and cultural monuments inundated with kids on school trips before winter arrives and many sights and services are closed over the long, cold winter. However, the Christmas markets and outdoor New Year celebrations are a wonderful time to see Bratislava at its decorated best.

ANNUAL EVENTS

January

Orthodox Christmas falls on 6 January and the season doesn't officially end until then.

February
Carnival is the season (Feb–Mar) of excess before and after belts are tightened for Lent. Experience music, food and performers on the streets of the Old Town.

March
Jam along to Living Blues, an annual international festival of rhythm and blues.

April
Take an alternate route to Bratislava from Devín Castle with a road race open to all ages, all abilities and all nationalities.

May
May Day heralds spring, the coming of summer and that the sap is rising ... The European Days of Summer cultural festival includes music, dance and recreational activities. International Museum & Gallery Day (18 May) sees Bratislava's venues open their doors for free.

● *The fountains of Hviezdoslavovo Square provide relief from the summer heat*

June

The International Water Sprite Festival wets the town around the Danube and Old Town. The Beer Festival (ⓦ www.junifest.sk) kicks off with cannon fire and hardly quietens afterwards.

July

Festival of Historical Combat, Music, Dance and Crafts at Devín Castle (July and August).

August

Events from the Summer Cultural Festival take place throughout the month (see page 14).

September

A superb three-day Coronation Festival takes Bratislava to its royal past as hundreds of people in period costume re-enact the Coronation procession. Enjoy festivities, eat roasts, marvel at knights, horsemen and fireworks as streets come alive with thousands of revellers.

October

More music with Bratislava Jazz Days (ⓦ www.bjd.sk). Meanwhile, the prestigious Bratislava Musical Festival (ⓦ www.bhsfestival.sk), which began 40 years ago, continues to collect international performers and accolades.

November

From late October, Bratislava's galleries, cafés and streets are covered in photography for Photography Month

(W www.fotofo.sk), Central Europe's oldest and most influential photo festival. The region raises glasses of *burčiak* (young wine) for the young wine festival (see page 110) and skirts, as it were, for the Flamenco Festival.

December

Traditional and warming food and drinks spice up the stalls and events of the Christmas markets, and concerts and fireworks herald the New Year at *Silvestre* (31 December). The Next Festival (W www.nextfestival.sk) showcases multimedia musicians, while the International Film Festival (W www.iffbratislava.sk) lights up Bratislava's screens.

NATIONAL PUBLIC HOLIDAYS
New Year and Day of Establishment of the Slovak Republic 1 Jan
Epiphany and Christmas of Orthodox Christians 6 Jan
May Day 1 May
Liberation of the Republic 8 May
St Cyril & St Methodius Day 5 July
Slovak National Uprising Day 29 Aug
Slovak Constitution Day 1 Sept
Our Lady of Seven Sorrows 15 Sept
All Saints' Day 1 Nov
Fight for Freedom & Democracy Day/Day of Students 17 Nov
Christmas Eve 24 Dec
Christmas Day 25 Dec
Boxing Day 26 Dec

Summer Cultural Festival

It's not the hills that are alive with the sound of music from late June to late September each year, it's the city, castle and river of Bratislava. The Summer Cultural Festival was inaugurated in 1975. Through the years, it has grown into a series of 200 presentations on 20 stages, featuring a cast of more than 1,500 from 20 countries. It's no wonder it attracts almost 70,000 visitors.

Diverse theatre, cinema, dance and music (from classical to gospel via blue grass, for example) attract audiences of all ages and interests. Sting once performed here, circus actors from Ukraine have fascinated kids and adults alike, and wine sampling adds to the atmosphere. Every summer, Bratislava offers a plethora of events, no matter your interests.

One of the highlights is Viva Musica!, a modern festival of classical music. Bratislava Castle courtyard hosts the Summer Shakespeare Festival. The corresponding Prague Castle Shakespeare Festival brings performances here and vice versa, putting the Bard's genius on a breathtaking stage. The castle concert hall echoes with the plaintive sounds of the Days of Organ Music and other concerts featuring renowned Slovak artists. The streets and squares of the Old Town bop to the beat of Celtic or Flamenco music, while the Old Town Hall and Zoo host popular children's events.

International and local visitors experience traditional Slovak folk music, culture, costumes and pastimes, such as fencing and dancing, while participants from countries as diverse as Taiwan and the USA introduce their cultural and musical heritage to the streets of Bratislava.

Slovak Constitution Day on 1 September is a particularly poignant day of proud celebration, but no matter how long or short a time you have, Bratislava defies you not to find its Summer Cultural Festival a feast for all senses.

● *A performance of the Slovak Philharmonic Orchestra*

History

Bratislava has hosted a settlement since the Iron Age, as the cliff site of Devín Castle was first settled. The local Celts were subdued by the Romans, who located their Limes Romanus defensive fortress at Devín in the 1st century AD, and the Slavs arrived in the late 5th century AD. By the 14th century, Bratislava had become one of the most important towns and castles of the Hungarian kingdom, and its fortified position held off sieges aplenty.

Bratislava's position on the border of three countries is testament to its muddled history. Rule had constantly fluctuated between Austria and Hungary with Polish and Jagiellonian kings entering the fray every now and then.

This rivalry between Hungary and Austria continued until 1526, when the Turks defeated the Hungarians and occupied Buda. The Hungarian kingdom became part of the Austrian (Habsburg) monarchy and in 1536 Bratislava (or Pressburg as it was known at the time) became the capital of Royal Hungary.

In 1808 Napoleon besieged Bratislava and bombed Devín. The 19th century saw a rise of the Slovak National Movement, with Ľudovít Štúr and friends codifying the Slovak language and leading the short-lived 1848 Revolution. Following the 1918 declaration of Czechoslovakia as an independent state, Bratislava revolted and was declared a free town. However, early 1919 saw Czech soldiers march on the city and bring it into the fold. Later that year, Bratislava officially became the city's name.

During World War II, Czechoslovakia was divided into two Nazi puppet states until liberation by the Red Army in April 1945. A few years later the Communist Party gained power.

Alexander Dubček, the Slovak politician briefly leader of Czechoslovakia (1968–9), attempted his famous reform of the communist regime (Prague Spring), but failed. His speech in Bratislava on 15 November 1989 inspired student demonstrations against the communists, and the Velvet Revolution took place on 19 November.

On 31 December 1992 Czechoslovakia was formally divided into two independent states. Since then Bratislava has been Slovakia's capital.

The 21st century has been a time of massive development since joining the EU in 2004. The city is now one of contrasts, with the historic core, communist showpiece projects and modern constructs making a stunning backdrop to cultural life.

⬤ *The earliest settlements were around Devín Castle*

Lifestyle

The Slovak Republic is still emerging from the yoke of the Communist Party, and there is a distinct difference in lifestyle between the older generation used to the pervasive power of the regime and the youth, who have few cultural differences to most people the world over of the same age.

This disparity is obvious in friendliness and language ability. Older people can seem cold and offer German as an alternate language, while young Bratislavans are global citizens with a growing knowledge of English. A cheery *dobrey deň* ('Hello', literally 'Good day') and *dovidenia* ('Goodbye') will help a smile light up a Slovak's face, and to really score points with the locals use *ahoj* (as sailors say) and *čau* (like the Italian *ciao*) for 'hello' and 'goodbye'. *Prosím* and *dakujem* complete your basic 'please' and 'thank you' vocabulary. Now, one oddity you'll have to get used to is that the Slovak word for 'yes' – *áno* – is shortened to *no*, which is rather confusing. 'No' is actually *nie*.

The traditional work day is 08.00–16.00, and breakfast is usually a moving feast of bread dipped in yoghurt or some savoury condiment – you'll see everyone eating on the trot. Lunch is, as dictated by the early breakfast, early. Restaurants and buffets run their excellent lunch deals from 11.00–15.00. The day's meals end with a hearty dinner at home, at a restaurant or at the pub.

The pub. Now, while the Slovakians, since their Velvet Divorce from the neighbouring Czechs, are no longer part of the No 1 beer drinking nation on the planet, drinking beer remains a popular activity with most age groups. Beer is consumed for breakfast, lunch and dinner, and it is proving difficult to persuade a nation of beer-drinkers that sipping an espresso at the same cost is a comparable experience. Pubs and bars are open all hours, are usually underground and usually serve food – even if only bar snacks in an attempt to sop up the litres of beer.

Slovaks are generally hospitable and friendly, unless you give them cause not to be – British stag parties take note.

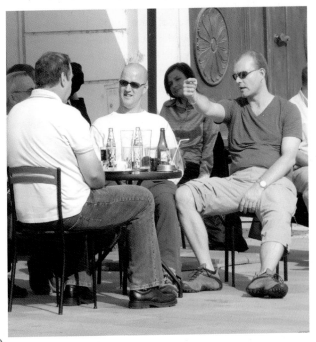

● *Relaxing with a beer is the national pastime*

Culture

In the past, it seems many people came to Bratislava on the traditional Grand Tour, on the way to or from Prague, Budapest and Vienna. However, people are now discovering that Bratislava is a destination in itself. Little wonder with such a chequered and extensive history!

The traditional folk music, costume and culture have remained an important facet of Slovakian life, and folkloric performances occur all over the country, usually during summer. Slovakia's royal and aristocratic heritage continues to attract tourists to Bratislava, and the region continues to produce objects and events aligned to these times. Modra is well known for traditional ceramic-making, and castles host historical festival days. Musically too, Bratislava has benefited hugely from Austria and Hungary's classical tradition. Both Mozart and Liszt performed in palaces here, while the composer J N Hummel was born here before moving to Austria to continue his work.

Austrians continue to flock to Bratislava for musical evenings, where the exterior beauty of the National Theatre and National Philharmonic buildings are mimicked by the myriad talents on stage, from chamber music to opera, drama and ballet. The prices are distinctly non-Western European, and a visit to the city should involve a foray into Bratislava's musical and theatrical heritage. Live music of all genres can be heard in clubs, restaurants and venues all over the city, but it is the summer months and festivals that really give these players their stage.

Bratislava has as many museums of various sizes as it has seen occupiers, and these fountains of historical fact exist in

SLOVENSKÉ NÁRODNÉ DIVADLO

The National Theatre has an international reputation for quality productions similarly historical houses, palaces and castles. The architecture of Bratislava, while not as classically golden as Prague's, has a complex Gothic, baroque and rococo heritage. That said, the Communists had no qualms about tearing down historical and religious sections of the city to make way for their calculated structural projects such as Nový most and Petržalka.

ⓘ All museums in the Slovak Republic are closed on Mondays.

Bratislava's art scene is not as renowned as its music scene, but there are numerous galleries showing religious and secular art from history as well as local and international contemporary artists. The National Gallery may not have any of the artistic wonders of the world, but the exhibits are a representative showcase of the porous borders of Bratislava's cultural identity.

Again, Bratislava is emerging from its 'older brother' syndrome and making its mark on the world's radar free from influence from Moscow or Prague. The city, though, is still trying to shake off the cloak of drab, grey Eastern Europe that Hollywood refuses to let go of.

◑ *Napoleon surveys Hlavné námestie (Main Square)*

Shopping

Bratislava's changing persona from provincial town to vibrant European capital city is obvious in the vast disparity of shopping opportunities. Local shops are very specific – although the veg shop, the meat shop and the bread shop did unite somewhat as the local *potraviny*, until the behemoth Tesco arrived and showed them exactly what a department store could be. This central Tesco now appears a mere throwback to Bratislava's past when you visit the ultra-modern malls of Aupark, Avion and Polus, which are popping up all over the suburbs and filled with the usual IKEAs, cinema multiplexes and retailers.

The historic centre is gradually attracting high-end retailers and, eventually, Bratislava will look like Paris or Prague, with the same boutiques and labels tempting shoppers. At the moment, there is no single area or street that is becoming the retail hub, although Obchodná – literally 'shops' in Slovak – is enticing regional chains to its newly pedestrianised quarter.

Souvenirs and folk objects (wood, ceramics, glass, wire sculptures) are doing brisk business for their unique value, and the market squares of old Pressburg continue a brisk trade today with stalls selling everything from tacky t-shirts to expertly crafted tin soldiers. If you are here at Christmas, then the large markets, though becoming more and more commercialised, should provide all your present-giving needs.

For a look at the way locals shop – although many stalls are run by Vietnamese – head to Miletičova open air market (Ⓝ Tram 8, 9, 14 to Záhradnícka, closed Sun) where you can buy anything from pickled cabbage to a pair of jeans.

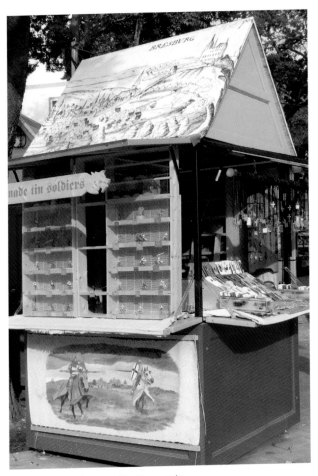

◉ The place to pick up an authentic souvenir

For a quality gift that almost everyone would love to receive, drop into one of Bratislava's wine shops for an excellent bottle of Slovak wine. Better still, visit the Small Carpathian wine country to buy at source – see page 110. Wherever you buy, it's a good idea to sample some variations.

USEFUL SHOPPING PHRASES

How much does ... cost?
Kol'ko stojí ...?
Koly-koh stow-gee?

I'm just looking. Thank you.
Len sa pozerám. Ďakujkem.
Lensa pozaam. Dyakuh-yem.

My size is ...
Mám číslo ...
Maam cheeslo ...

I'll like ...
Potrebujem ...
Poh-trebuhyem ...

Do you accept credit cards?
Môžem platiť úverovou kartou?
Muo-zhem plah-tyity ooveh-rovohw kar-tohw?

Eating & drinking

The days of Italian cuisine being a plate of spaghetti with ketchup and a vegetarian menu consisting of fried cheese are long gone as Bratislava's palate broadens to involve all variety of ethnic, haute and fusion cuisine.

Bars, cafés and restaurants come in all shapes, sizes and kitchens, but you will find most places serve food – from a little something to go with your beer such as *utopenec* (pickled sausage) to half a spit-roasted pig. Slovak cuisine is traditionally non-vegetarian, heavy, hearty and rib-sticking. The national dish is a delicious mix of *halušky* (potato dumplings) with *bryndza* (a sheep milk cheese) scattered with fried onion. A less rich version is *strapačky*, which is *halušky* with sauerkraut. In addition to the usual pork, chicken and beef, local cuisine makes great use of duck, goose and game, usually in rich gravy and served with dumplings. The autumnal feast of *husacina* (stone-oven-roast goose) served with *burčiak* (young wine) is not to be missed if you are here for the season.

Slovak fast food consists of unsophisticated fried items: *lokše* are potato pancakes served sweet or as an accompaniment to

---

PRICE RATING
Price ratings in this book are based on the approximate price of a three-course meal for one person, excluding drinks but including tax.
£ = up to 300 SLK   **££** = 300–1,000 SLK
£££ = above 1,000 SLK

dinner and slathered with dripping. *Langoše*, a greasy fried dough pizza dolloped with ketchup and cheese, seems only to be savoured by locals, but the ubiquitous *pirôžky* windows serve up a sweet doughnut, perfect for breakfast or snack for a very reasonable price. One glaring odd man out in unhealthy fast food is the Slovak vegetarian buffet, where you join the queue, order, pay, then take your plate. Try **Divesta** (£ ⓐ Laurínska 8 🕓 11.00–15.00) where the long line quickly dwindles.

Bageta, or *richman*, are the mayonnaise-filled sandwiches you'll see folk munching on all over the place. A good spot for these are the windows on Mariánska, which seem to be open all the time – including weekends.

⬤ *Just one of the myriad brands of beer consumed in Slovakia*

Once you know what to eat, there's the question of what to wash it down with. The fast answer is beer. Whether it's Czech, Slovak or German, beer is everywhere, in glasses large and small, at prices exorbitant or unbelievably low. However, the region's wine heritage is one of Bratislava's best-kept secrets, and many traditional and contemporary restaurants have a fine selection of local wines.

Traditional spirits – homemade is the best – such as *slivovice* (from plums) or *borovička* (from juniper berries) are the shots

NA ZDRAVIE!

If you are eager to sample some Slovak beers, you'll need to know which ones are homebrewed. The only beer brewed in Bratislava is Stein, although you'd never know it as Zlatý Bažant (Golden Pheasant, made by Heineken in Nitra) and Šariš (made by giants SAB Miller) are the most common taps you'll find in bars in the city. Other Slovak beers are Steiger, Tatran, Urpín, Popper, Hordan, Corgoň and Smedne Mnich (Thirsty Monk), while Topvar sponsors many local beer gardens, such as **Prešporská kúria/Pizzéria Niki** (£ ⓐ Dunajská 21 ⓛ 09.00–22.00 (10.00–22.00 on Sat & Sun).

Beers listed as 10° (e.g. Czech Gambrinus) have less alcohol than 12° versions. Also, bear in mind that *svelte* is lager and *tmavé* is dark beer. If you fancy trying Diesel, be aware that it's a mix of light beer and coke.

See ⓦ www.kamnapivo.sk for a list (in Slovak but with icons) of some of the best beer places in town.

you'll be offered by new Slovak friends. They are a tad harsh, so you may want to opt for the subtler herbal taste of Becherovka – although it is Czech. In the winter, everyone warms up with numerous cups of *svařák* (mulled wine that comes in red and white varieties) or *grog* (hot rum together with a bag of *pečené gaštany* – roast chestnuts).

USEFUL DINING PHRASES

A table for two, please
Stôl pre dvoch, prosim
Stwal pre dvock, proh-seem

I'm a vegetarian
(Ja) som vegetarián
(Jah) som veghe-tahryiaan

breakfast
raňajky
ranyai-kih

lunch
obed
obed

dinner
večera
vecheh-rah

The bill, please
Učet, procim
Oochet, proh-seem

I would like a beer please
Jedo pivo, prosim
Yednoh pih-voh, proh-seem

Entertainment & nightlife

The word 'Partyslava' might not trip off the tongues of today's visitors, but if Bratislavans and tourists (as well as those entrepreneurs developing more and ever varying venues for the party to spread) continue, then Bratislava will have acquired yet another name in its long history.

The key to Bratislava's nightlife is that it doesn't necessarily happen at night. As is infinitely noticeable, as soon as winter transforms into spring, Bratislava morphs into a sea of outdoor tables and beer gardens and, whenever the sun shines, people hit these havens and begin the day's entertainment. Similarly, in winter, the best way to beat the chill is with a little *après-ski*, even if it is strictly *avant* ...

Café bars, which usually shut around 24.00, provide the warm-up party, with relaxed atmosphere and food if you haven't made reservations somewhere. The chic cocktail bars and restaurants kick off later in the evening as people converge on the hotspots with DJs where the party gets started (and, for those who lack stamina, ends!). Legendary clubs such as Subclub and Cirkus Barok still attract the crowds with new pretenders Trafo, Sparx and UFO fuelling a more cocktail-gargling sharp-dressed crowd.

Bratislava's venues all seem to be moulded in the arty, grandmother's den of eclecticism or the new, sleek, design spaces – with little in between. Luckily, the city is easy to traverse on foot and you can descend into any open door and decide whether or not it's for you. However, new hotspots Harley's and Coyote Ugly are a taxi ride away and luckily don't disappoint.

⬤ *Bratislavan street entertainer*

There aren't many specific live music venues, but restaurants often have some folk or jazz musicians to add to the atmosphere. Bratislava is on the tour of visiting international artists, e.g. Duran Duran and The Prodigy, who usually play Incheba Expo (ⓐ Viedenská cesta 3–7 ❶ 02 6727 2400 ⓦ www.incheba.sk) or PKO (ⓐ Nábr arm Gen Ľ'Svobodu 3 ❶ 02 5910 3101 ⓦ www.bkis.sk).

❶ To check what's on around Bratislava, visit ⓦ www.fanvbratislave.sk (which is the poster with live music, cinema, etc. you see in venues all over the city) or ⓦ www.booom.sk (which is a clubbing what's on guide).

If gambling is your bag, then the sublime Philharmonic building houses the Reduta Casino, while the Regency Casino is in the Crowne Plaza Hotel.

In 2005, the *New York Times* named Bratislava as one of its top gay destinations and while the scene isn't big, it is apparently beautiful. Try a new place, 4 Pink's (ⓐ Župné nám 3 ⓦ www.4pinks.sk) and an old favourite, Apollon (ⓐ Panenská 24

ON SONG

Slovakia and the Slovak National Theatre have produced some internationally acclaimed opera stars, including tenor Peter Dvorský who performed at Vienna's State Opera and La Scala before returning to Bratislava. Lucia Poppova debuted in Bratislava before popping over to Vienna, as did fellow *coloraturas* Edita Gruberová.

Ⓦ www.apollon-gay-club.sk). Both websites are in English, as is
Ⓦ www.gay.sk. A relaxed mixed hangout is Café U Anjelov
(Ⓐ Laurinská 19 Ⓦ www.anjeli.sk).

And now for the other end of the sex spectrum: the Great
British Stag Party. As Eastern Europe opens up via low-cost
airlines, the stag party wreaks its noisy, drunken havoc on
unsuspecting cities hosting cheap beer and beautiful women.
Bratislava has become one of these destinations, and while the
money these groups of similarly dressed men bring is an
important part of the nation's GDP, the behaviour that comes
with it cancels the financial benefits.

❶ The British Embassy has agreed with the government that
any British national breaking a law will be deported – so be
warned and behave.

PLAY THAT GUITAR!
The Dobro, the famous and distinctive-sounding resonator
guitar, was designed in 1928 by Slovakian Ján Dopjera and
his brothers. Dobro is a contraction of Dopjera Brothers
and means 'good' in their native Slovak language. In recent
decades, the Dobro has been used by the Eagles, Lynyrd
Skynyrd and Dire Straits.

Sport & relaxation

The great outdoors is a big draw for Slovaks, due probably to the long, cold winter. That said, the cold, or snow at least, is the draw whether the slope is in the High Tatras Mountains or Bratislava's Koliba. Then there is hiking and biking, popular activities along both the banks of the Danube and Koliba (see page 97).

❶ You can hire bikes in Bratislava but with some difficulty. An agency called Luka hires them out, but it's best to ask at the tourist office (page 136) for contact details.

In the summer, if you need to cool down, head to Malý Draždiak, a lake south of Petržalka. Take bus 95 to Šintavská. In addition to indoor pools in the larger hotels, Aupark has the super Aulandia Aqua & Spa Paradise, which provides separate areas for adults and kids to pamper themselves and have some fun – both inside and out – with pools, slides, spa, sauna and massage.
Aupark ❷ Einsteinova 18 ❸ 02 6820 1031 Ⓦ www.aulandia.sk
🕓 10.00–22.00
In town, the lovely Czech import of **Sabai** offers Thai massage, foot massage, etc. ❷ Laurinská 4 ❸ 02 5924 1133 Ⓦ www.sabai.sk
🕓 10.00–22.00

SPECTATOR SPORTS
Ice hockey is the national sport of the Slovak Republic and, as such, ticket prices are low and quality of play is high. Games are usually on Tuesdays, Fridays and Sundays. Tickets cost 100–200 SLK.

HC Slovan Bratislava ⓐ Odbojárov 9 ⓣ 02 4445 6500
ⓦ www.hcslovan.sk ⓝ Tram: 2, 4, 6

The other national sport is football. Bratislava has two teams, and tickets are ridiculously cheap for local games (30–80 SLK). For international games, though, prices are a higher 500–1,000 SLK.

ŠK Slovan Bratislava ⓐ Viktora Tegelhofa 4 ⓣ 02 4463 6363
ⓦ www.slovanfutbal.com ⓝ Tram: 2, 4, 6

ŠK Inter Bratislava ⓐ Junácka 10 ⓣ 02 4445 5889
ⓦ www.askinter.sk/futbal ⓝ Tram: 2, 4, 6

If you fancy a flutter, you need to find the hippodrome for some horse racing at Petržalka. Races are usually on Sunday afternoon Apr–Oct. Tickets are 40/20 SLK.

Závodisko Bratislava ⓐ Starohájska 29 ⓣ 02 6241 1504
ⓦ www.zavodisko.sk ⓝ Bus: 198

🔺 *Climbing the walls in the Janko Kral park*

Accommodation

Bratislava is notorious for expensive accommodation, be it peak season or not. That said, as with everything else in this burgeoning capital city, more options are becoming available. Last-minute deals can be obtained from the tourist office and usually comprise private rooms in residential houses.

HOTELS & GUEST HOUSES

City Hostel £ With all en suite rooms and no dorms, this isn't a hostel except in price. New, clean and very sufficient.
ⓐ Obchodná 38 ⓣ 02 5263 6041 ⓦ www.cityhostel.sk
ⓝ Tram: 1, 5, 6, 7, 9

Best Western Hotel West ££ Standard rooms but with rural pursuits plus pool and sauna. With a restaurant on site.
ⓐ Kamzíkov vrch, Koliba ⓣ 02 5478 8692 ⓦ www.hotel-west.sk
ⓝ Bus: 203

Castle Club ££ Small, homely B&B on the steep path up to Bratislava Castle with WiFi. It also has numerous apartments, all

> ## PRICE RATING
> Gradings are based on the approximate price of an en suite room for two people in high season, including tax.
> **£** = up to 1,000 SLK
> **££** = 1,000–4,000 SLK
> **£££** = above 4,000 SLK

central with all services and appliances included and discounts available. ⓐ Zámocké schody 4 ⓦ www.stayslovakia.sk

Chez David ££ Small, personal service with less-than-luxurious rooms and one apartment. Location and the restaurant are the real draws. ⓐ Zámocká 13 ⓣ 02 5441 3824 ⓦ www.chezdavid.sk ⓝ Tram: 1, 5, 6, 7, 9

Hotel Kyjev ££ A communist landmark and slice of history served to you with little style but a big smile. ⓐ Rajská 2 ⓣ 02 5964 1111 ⓦ www.kyjev-hotel.sk ⓝ Tram: 4, 6, 7, 11, 14; Bus: 202, 205

Hotel Matyšak ££ New hotel with large rooms, apartments with terrace, free internet and a wine cellar with 4,000 bottles beneath your room. Excellent. ⓐ Pražská 15 ⓣ 02 2063 4001 ⓦ www.hotelmatysak.sk ⓝ Bus: 204, 206, 209, 212

Hotel Spirit ££ Wacky avant-garde architecture and healing foods, relaxation pyramid, gallery, apartments and dorm behind the railway station. Unique yet sparse. ⓐ Vančurova 1 ⓣ 02 5477 7561 ⓦ www.hotelspirit.sk ⓝ Tram: 1, 2 3, 8; Bus: 210

Ibis ££ You know what you're getting with an Ibis, and this is no different to the usual identikit experience. ⓐ Zámocká 38 ⓣ 02 5929 2000 ⓦ www.ibis-bratislava.sk ⓝ Tram: 1, 5, 6, 7, 9

Koliba-Expo ££ Small but perfectly formed classic Slovak wooden chalet with Heidi-inspired rooms and apartments in

🔺 *The Radisson Savoy Carlton occupies a prime historic location*

the mountains. A short taxi ride from the city centre but a world away from the hustle and bustle. ⓐ Kamzíkov vrch, Koliba ⓣ 02 5477 1764 ⓦ www.koliba-expo.sk ⓝ Bus: 203

Old City Hotel ££ Good deal for basic, sometimes noisy, rooms in the Old Town. No lift, three floors, under 10s stay free. ⓐ Michalská 2 ⓣ 02 5443 0258 ⓦ www.oldcityhotel.sk

Crowne Plaza £££ Huge hotel with all mod cons opposite the Presidential Palace plus fusion restaurant, casino, pool and gym. ⓐ Hodžovo nám 2 ⓣ 02 5934 8111 ⓦ www.crowneplaza.com

Hotel Antares £££ Lovely converted villa in residential area with terrace, luxurious rooms and relax centre. ⓐ Šulekova 15 ⓣ 02 5464 8971 ⓦ www.hotelantares.sk ⓝ Bus: 203, 207, 208

Hotel Danube £££ Views, well-appointed rooms and a fitness centre situated aptly along the river. ⓐ Rybné nám 1 ⓣ 02 5934 0000 ⓦ www.hoteldanube.com ⓝ Tram: 1, 11, 12, 14

Hotel Devín £££ Not at Devín Castle, but with fitness centre, WiFi, classically styled, fully appointed rooms in the historic centre and on the Danube. ⓐ Riečna 4 ⓣ 02 5443 3640 ⓦ www.hoteldevin.sk ⓝ Tram: 1, 11, 12, 14

Hotel Dukla £££ Traditional hotel with upgraded rooms and services. Worth staying for the game restaurant alone. ⓐ Dulovo nám 1 ⓣ 02 5596 8933 ⓦ www.hoteldukla.sk ⓝ Bus: 50, 82, 85

Hotel Hradná brána £££ Enjoy a rural retreat at this new and very comfortable 11-room hotel with relax centre and restaurant. ⓐ Slovanské nábr 15, Devín ⓣ 02 6010 2513 ⓦ www.hotelhb.sk ⓝ Bus: 29

Hotel Marrol's £££ A member of Small Luxury Hotels of the World and it is – leather furniture in the lobby, luxury in every room. ⓐ Tobrucká 4 ⓣ 02 5778 4600 ⓦ www.hotelmarrols.sk ⓝ Tram: 1, 11, 12, 14

Hotel Perugia £££ Small and central with personalised service and an excellent Slovak restaurant. ⓐ Zelená 5 ⓣ 02 5443 1818 ⓦ www.perugia.sk

Radisson SAS Carlton £££ A new hotel for a historical location that cannot be bettered. Pure luxury. ⓐ Hviezdoslavovo nám 3 ⓣ 02 5939 0000 ⓦ www.radissonsas.com ⓝ Tram: 1, 4, 11, 12, 14

HOSTELS
Downtown Backpackers £ Popular and busy, it has character and dark corners. ⓐ Panenská 31 ⓣ 02 5464 1191 ⓦ www.backpackers.sk ⓝ Bus: 81, 91, 93, 208

Patio Hostel £ Rooms and dorms with shared bathrooms. Cleanliness fluctuates but free internet and cool folk are a draw. Strictly no smoking. ⓐ Špitálska 35 ⓣ 02 5292 5797 ⓦ www.patiohostel.com ⓝ Tram: 4, 6, 7, 11, 14; Bus: 202, 205

THE BEST OF BRATISLAVA

Bratislava draws you in with its historic centre, imposing castle, renowned river, and buzzing cultural and night life. Then, if you stay a little longer, you discover so much more.

TOP 10 ATTRACTIONS

- **Bratislavský hrad (Bratislava Castle)** The seat of the Hungarian kings and queens and summer home of Maria Theresa, Bratislava Castle is now a wonderful museum with temporary and permanent exhibits (see page 77).

- **Devín Castle** Border outpost of the Roman Empire and cultural heart of the Slovak nation, there has been a settlement here since 4000 BC (see pages 93 and 96–97).

- **Stará radnica (Old Town Hall)** A private house donated to the city, then added to over the centuries to form the historic heart of city life and Bratislava's oldest and possibly most interesting museum (see page 70).

- **Michalská brána (St Michael's Gate & Tower)** The only surviving gate of the city's medieval fortifications, the tower is now a museum and affords spectacular views of Bratislava and beyond (see page 67).

- **Konkatedrála sv Martina (St Martin's Cathedral)**
  Bratislava's largest and most important church. Today, classical concerts, a crypt and skeletal remains beneath a glass floor draw spectators (see page 66).

- **Slovenská Národná galerie (Slovak National Gallery)**
  Permanent and temporary exhibitions of Slovak and European art housed in the old water barracks and a modern annexe (see page 85).

- **The Korzo** The name for the pedestrian section, where you can lose yourself in the streets, alleys and courtyards of Bratislava's Old Town and castle environs (see page 62).

- **Slavín Monument** Before the Soviets wrested power from an independent Czechoslovakia, the Red Army liberated the city from the Nazis in 1945. This is the monument to their fallen Soviet comrades (see page 100).

- **Ice hockey** The Slovaks excel at their national sport and were World Champions in 2002. Games are cheap and thrilling – whether you know the rules or not (see page 35).

- **The Danube** Wander along the river, then walk (or waltz) across the Danube to Janka Kráľa gardens. Don't miss Nový most, as if you could (see page 83).

◆ *Detail from a door in the Old Town*

Here's a brief guide to the best Bratislava can offer, depending on how much time you have available.

HALF-DAY: BRATISLAVA IN A HURRY

Wander around the historic centre and visit the Bratislava Castle grounds (for free) or take a look inside the castle itself. A walking or vintage car tour, chaffeur driven, will allow you to see the maximum amount in a limited time. Ask at the tourist office for details (see page 136).

1 DAY: TIME TO SEE A LITTLE MORE

Start your day with the above tour. Then relax in one of the city's many eateries. Wash down your lunch with a beer or glass of wine, then make your way to Devín Castle (see pages 93, 96–97), the historical and cultural heart of Slovakia. Alternatively, visit a museum locally – either the Old Town Hall or the Slovak National Gallery.

2–3 DAYS: SHORT CITY-BREAK

This amount of time will give you plenty of opportunity to explore some of the city's palaces and museums. What's more, you'll be able to get fully acquainted with both Bratislava and Devín Castles (see pages 77–78 and 93, 96–97). Both have wonderful museums and interesting surroundings. The views around Devín particularly are breathtaking. If you still have time, take a trip to the Small Carpathians for some wine tasting. An encounter with the beautiful Slovak countryside and the fabulous Červený kameň castle will fill a whole day.

LONGER: ENJOYING BRATISLAVA TO THE FULL

With even more time on your hands, you'll really be able to get to know the cobbled streets, parks, castle, palaces and museums of the city. Head out and explore the surroundings, beginning with Devín Castle. Then partake of some rural activities on Koliba, whether it is winter or summer. A Carpathian wine tour makes a great day out, as does a visit to Vienna or even Budapest.

BRATISLAVA CITY CARD

This discount card is available from any of the tourist information offices (see page 136). The card allows unlimited travel on all of Bratislava's public transport. It also gives a free and informative walking tour of the Old Town. The card costs 200 SLK for one day, 300 SLK for two days and 370 SLK for three days.

⬤ *Awe-inspiring Devin Castle*

Something for nothing

Bratislava is still cheap, but prices have risen since joining the EU, and when Slovakia adopts the euro, prices will probably align themselves with Western Europe.

With summer festivals, concerts and activities occurring in many public spaces, finding something for nothing isn't difficult if you ever tire of just walking around Bratislava's winding streets and beautiful parks observing ornate details and quirky facts. In addition, museum entrance fees are nominal, so seeing the city's rich cultural history is within everybody's means. Museums are free on International Museum & Gallery Day (18 May). Also, the extensive grounds around Bratislava Castle are free, as is visiting Slavín Monument and venturing to the top of the Kamzík TV Tower, both of which afford a superb vista of the city illustrating the contrast of new and old architecture.

The Slovenská sporiteľňa galerie (@ Zelená 2 ❶ 02 5977 9102 ❷ 12.00–18.00) is the only collection of fine arts outside of state museums and galleries, and it's free. Various media are exhibited from usually Slovak contemporary artists.

A delightful find on the square at the Old Town end of Obchodná (❷ Hurbanovo nám) is a group of objects on the small lawn that appear at first glance to be a piece of wood and a manhole cover perhaps. The Dancing Bells are actually nine metal panels forming a carillon to be stepped on to produce music. They are fascinating, especially if someone actually has some musical talent. Check out the wobbly bench, too.

The huge outdoor Miletičova market (Tram 8, 9, 14 to Záhradnícka, closed Sun) is a great place to see the real

Bratislava. Fresh produce grown by the sellers themselves, produce pickled by them – you get the picture. Arts and crafts, plus food, clothes and objects you might never have thought to find at a market. Free to window shop – as it were – and cheap if you decide to buy something.

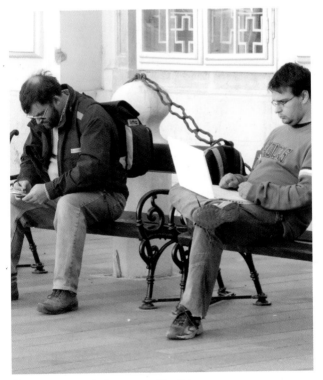

◆ *Wi-Fi spots are springing up around the city*

When it rains

Rain isn't necessarily the reason you'll want to head inside while touring Bratislava: plummeting temperatures and horizontal sleet are often a deciding factor for winter visitors. By far the most accessible retreat in times of adverse weather conditions is the nearest cosy bar or café. Hot chocolate, mulled wine or a beer will brighten any day and one of the beauties of Bratislava is that no matter where you are when the heavens open, you're never far from a bar/café of some version.

Another obvious refuge is a museum or gallery, picking one of the larger ones to extend your shelter time. The National Gallery has rooms and corridors aplenty and an extended visit to the Old Town Hall exhibits will fill any dreary afternoon. Another option is the vintage car tour, where you can sit in comfort and have a chauffeured trip round the city (❶ 0903 302 817 Ⓦ www.presporacik.sk ❹ Apr–Oct only). It's only 30 minutes long, but perfect for an April shower.

If you've seen enough culture, you can always head out to shop till you drop at one of the modern malls where non-shopaholics have options too. Try bowling, or immerse yourself in an alternate reality by taking in a movie. The mall multiplexes show all the usual Hollywood blockbusters so check the schedules at Aupark (Ⓦ www.palacecinemas.sk) and Polus (Ⓦ www.istropoliscinemacenter.sk). Note that kids' movies are usually dubbed. The central Kino Mladošt (❹ Hviezdoslavovo nám 17 ❶ 02 5443 5000) shows quality European films, which means subtitles will only be in the Slovak language. And FK

(Film Klub) Charlie (ⓐ Špitálska 4 ❶ 02 5296 8994) hosts quality films and festivals such as the notable One World/ Jeden Svét.

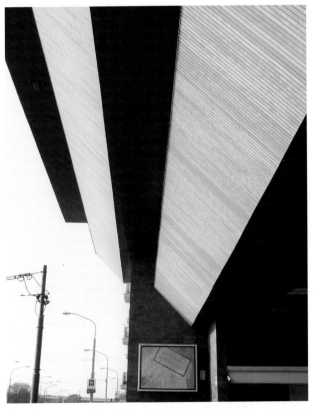

🔺 *Behind the austere façade of the National Gallery lie interesting art exhibits*

On arrival

TIME DIFFERENCES

Slovakia follows Central European Time (CET). From late
March to late October the clocks are put ahead one hour.
In the Slovak summer, at 12.00, the time elsewhere is as
follows.

Australia Eastern Standard Time 20.00, Central Standard Time
19.30, Western Standard Time 18.00
New Zealand 22.00
South Africa 12.00
UK 11.00
USA and Canada Newfoundland Time 07.30, Atlantic Canada
Time 07.00, Eastern Time 06.00, Central Time 05.00, Mountain
Time 04.00, Pacific Time 03.00, Alaska 02.00

ARRIVING
By air
Domestic and international flights use Bratislava's Letisko MR
Štefánik airport, which lies 9 km (5½ miles) northeast of the city
(ⓐ Ivanská cesta ❶ 02 3303 3353/4857 3353
ⓦ www.airportbratislava.sk). The airport currently has two
terminals: Terminal A for departures and Terminal B for arrivals.
A third terminal, C, also for arrivals, is under construction.

   Taxis are renowned for overcharging, so arrange a price first
or make sure you have a reputable driver. Savvy travellers often
pick up taxis from the departure terminal, where drivers have
already made the trip out and might not be as keen to rip

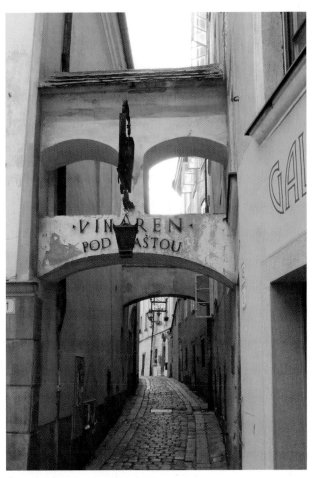

● *Exploring the alleyways of the Old Town*

visitors off. Expect to pay around 450 SLK for the 15–25 minute journey into the city.

Bus 61 runs from the airport to Hlavná stanica (central train station) every 10–20 minutes from 04.45–23.45 (23.05 from the train station). There you change onto another bus/trolley to take you into the city centre from there.

By rail

Bratislava Hlavná stanica (central train station) (ⓐ Predstaničné nám 1 ⓦ www.zsr.sk/www.slovakrail.sk) provides connections around Slovakia and to and from various neighbouring countries. The train station is well linked by public transport into the city.

By coach

Autobusova stanica, aka Bratislava's coach station (ⓐ Mlynské Nivy ⓣ 0972 222 222), is linked to the city centre via trolley bus. Numbers 202, 205, 208 are the most commonly used. Good bus and coach links from here connect with all of Bratislava and neighbouring countries.

Driving

With trams, buses and trolley buses, pedestrianised zones and Bratislava's infamous traffic jams, driving here especially at peak times is a nightmare for the uninitiated. Car parks are common and prices not too high. Some hotels provide parking spaces.

FINDING YOUR FEET

Although it uses the same alphabet as English, the Slovak language is tricky for foreign tongues to get around, so asking for directions can be a chore. Bratislava remains a fairly parochial city despite the ongoing developments and some Bratislavans can seem a cold and unfriendly people. These days, though, you'll find more locals speaking English and the older generations will always try German or merely point.

ORIENTATION

The Old Town and some connecting streets are pedestrianised, and walking around (probably in circles for a while at least) is the best way for orientation. Bratislava Castle is an excellent landmark, as is the Dunaj (River Danube) itself. Tram lines closest to the Old Town stop at Kapucínska, Hviezdoslavovo nám (National Theatre) and Kammené nám (Tesco). For trolleybuses, Hodžovo nám (the Presidential Palace) and Rajská (Tesco again) are the central stops.

IF YOU GET LOST, TRY ...

Do you speak English?
Hovoríte po anglicky?
Havoh-ree-tyeh poh ahnglits-kih?

How do I get to ...?
Ako sa dostanem do ...?
Akoh sa dostah-nyem doh ...?

Where's ...?
Kde je ...?
Gdyeh yeh ...?

Can you show me (on the map)?
Môžete mi ukázať (na mape)?
Muo-zhetyeh mih uh-kaazaty (nah mapeh)?

Pekná cesta
Nový záhon
Vozovňa Krasňany
Nám. Biely kríž
Mladá garda

Komisárky (3) (5)

Zlaté Piesky (2) (4)

Rožňavská
Vajnorská

ŽST Vinohrady
(7) (11) (17)

Jurajov dvor
Magnetová
Odborárska

Nové
Město

Riazanská
Pionierska
Ursínyho
Račianske mýto
Vazovova

Žatišie

ZST Nové Mesto (1)

Polus City Center
Nová doba
Odbojárov

Slovanet

(8) (9) (14)

Astronomická

Záhradicka   Pri jazere
Trnavské mýto

Ružnov

Legionárska
Odboráske nám.
Americké nám.
Mariánska

Floriánske
nám

Staré
Město

Kamenné nám.

Šafárikovo nám. (12)

Tram lines
— 1   — 8
— 2   — 9
— 3   — 11
— 4   — 12
— 5   — 13
— 7   — 14
                 — 17

Service stops in only
in direction shown

GETTING AROUND
Tram, bus & trolleybus

The easiest way around is on foot, as Bratislava isn't very big. Once away from the hilly castle section, it remains fairly flat and of course a large portion is dedicated to pedestrians. For the Old Town, it's walking only, as public transport runs a ring around these small, winding and often cobbled streets. If you have a hotel in the Old Town, taxis might drop you at the door.

There are 13 tram lines, 11 trolleybuses (which are trackless trams) and 77 bus lines. Some 18 night bus routes run from 24.00 to 05.00. A superb website (ⓦ www.imhd.sk) lists all routes and times, and is in English. The main interchanges are Hodžovo nám, Nový most and Kamenné nám. As Bratislava's entire transport system is integrated, one ticket will cover all forms of transport. That said, you must buy tickets before getting on board. You'll get these from a ticket shop (at the bus and train stations, for example), *tabak* kiosk or yellow vending machine. Additionally, you must validate the ticket by inserting it into the orange franking machines by the doors of trams and buses. If a tram or trolleybus door doesn't open, push the button above the doors.

Tickets cost 10 SLK for a 10-minute journey, 18 SLK for 30 minutes (45 minutes at off-peak times) and 22 SLK for 60 minutes (off-peak 90 minutes). Reduced fares for the tickets are 7, 9 and 11 SLK respectively. A 24-hour ticket costs 90 SLK and a week's ticket is 310 SLK, with various denominations in between. These are worth getting, as they'll pay the way to Devín Castle, for example. What's more, if you have no ticket or one that's not validated, you face a fine of 1,400 SLK.

🛈 Make sure the ticket inspector shows his credentials before you start paying out.
🛈 Public transport is free with the Bratislava City Card (see page 45).
🛈 On public holidays, the Sunday timetable operates.

Taxi

As usual, be careful when hailing a passing taxi – unless you know how much your journey should cost. Company names, rather than an unmarked car with a yellow taxi light, are safer and cheaper. Hotel taxis are more expensive. Do not hesitate to ask the restaurant or venue you are at to call a taxi for you. Alternatively, try these:

MB Taxi 🛈 02 16916 or 0902 916 916 (mobile)
Super Taxi 🛈 02 16616 or 0903 616 616 (mobile)

CAR HIRE

Booking a hire car with your plane ticket often saves money, although firms have offices in Bratislava, too. You'll find the following in the arrivals hall:

Alimex 🛈 02 4328 4582 🌐 www.alimex.sk
Avis 🛈 02 4341 0709 🌐 www.avis.sk
Europcar 🛈 02 4926 2637 🌐 www.europcar.sk
Hertz 🛈 02 4329 1482 🌐 www.hertz.sk
Sixt 🛈 02 4824 5178 🌐 www.sixt.sk

Car

A car is extremely useful for excursions around Bratislava, although there may be some arguments on the designated driver for touring the wine region. However, if you are staying in the city for sightseeing, park the car and wander on foot.

Boat

Bratislava sits prettily on the Danube between Budapest and Vienna, both of which have river connections. You can also journey up and down the Danube on a shorter sightseeing tour or a dinner cruise. The Danube does have low water problems, which could postpone or even cancel your trip. Cruises cease in winter.

LOD ⓐ Fajnorovo nábrežie 2 ⓣ 02 5293 2226 ⓦ www.lod.sk
Twin City Liner ⓐ Rázusovo nábrežie ⓦ www.twincityliner.com

▶ *Ancient and modern – a view over the Bratislava rooftops*

Old Town

The winding streets of Bratislava's Old Town are a walk into history, with beautiful buildings featuring commemoration plaques to such luminaries as Mozart, Liszt and Pálffy. The lanes meander around the central areas of Hlavné námestie (Main Square), and Hviezdoslavovo nám, and are bordered by Staromestká street leading to Nový most (New Bridge) towards the castle, Michalská brána (St Michael's Gate) towards Obchodná street, Nám SNP, Štúrova street and, of course, the Danube. The *korzo* (as the area is known) has no public transport – except trams passing by the National Theatre – but it is small and perfect to explore for hours on foot, especially the not-yet-renovated area around Prepoštská and Kapitulská streets.

SIGHTS & ATTRACTIONS

Hlavné námestie (Main Square)

The main square was and is the hub of life in the city. In the past, this area was used as the main market (check out the yard sticks and butcher's knife on the left of the entrance to the Old Town Hall), as well as for executions and celebrations.

The fountain at the heart of the square was commissioned by Maximilian II in 1572 after fire swept through the square. It is known as the Maximilian Fountain, or the Roland Fountain as Max is depicted in full knight's armour à la Roland.

It is said that, on New Year's Eve, Roland will turn around and even walk! But we have yet to see it, as there are conditions

attached to the miracle that have precluded its occurrence –
one is that a sober, Bratislavan-born virgin be present.

Hviezdoslavovo námestie (Hviezdoslav Square)

The largest city square was the location of the moat filled in by
Maria Theresa to allow for extensive construction when the city
walls were torn down. It is lined with restaurants, cafés and
bars, has a free ice rink in the winter, a giant chessboard in
summer, saw George W Bush address the nation, is home to the
German and US Embassies, the National Theatre and
Philharmonic buildings, and it hosts the Christmas market.

⬥ *Hlavné námestie, the focal point of the Old Town*

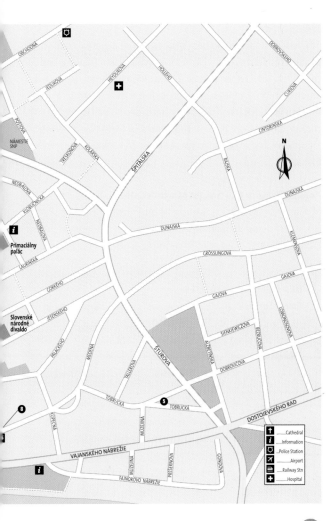

Legend	
✝	....Cathedral
i	....Information
🔄	....Police Station
✈	....Airport
▤	....Railway Stn
✚	....Hospital

Primaciálny palác

Slovenské národné divadlo

Jewish Memorial

The Jewish quarter and beautiful synagogue were demolished in 1969 to make way for Nový most, which didn't endear the modern bridge to the people. The etching of the synagogue on smooth marble appears to have restored its location as it merges with adjacent buildings' reflections. The Holocaust monument says on it 'Remember' in both Slovakian and Hebrew. Hannukah and other holidays continue to be celebrated here.
🅐 Rudnavovo nám.

Konkatedrála sv Martina (St Martin's Cathedral)

St Martin's Cathedral is the largest and most important of Bratislava's church buildings: Pope John Paul II celebrated and Liszt conducted mass here. Construction began in 1221, but it

BRATISLAVA'S STATUES

Hans Christian Andersen travelled through Bratislava in 1840 and this statue of the master storyteller illustrates his imagination (🅐 Hviezdoslavovo nám, opposite the US Embassy). Unfortunately, someone stole the cute ugly duckling from his feet, but the sculptor has promised a replacement.

The top-hatted Schöner Naci statue (🅐 Rybárska brána) is of Ignac Lamar, a local dandy who, denied his one true love, wandered the city giving flowers to women and sweets to children until his death in 1967. He too was vandalised – by a British stag party – and is now watched over by CCTV.

wasn't consecrated until 1452 due to wars and lack of funds. Between 1563 and 1830, its hallowed halls saw 19 Hungarian kings and queens crowned, and the 300-g (10-oz) gilt crown atop its 85-m (279-ft) tall tower is a replica of their crown. Its Gothic interior holds four chapels, a crypt (take a torch), and a spectacular statue by Juraj Raphael Donner depicting St Martin.

The cathedral was built into the city walls. You can see a remaining section opposite the entrance, and this placement made it impossible to have the entrance facing the altar as is usual. Concerts are regularly held here and although you cannot hear the rumblings from the busy road, you can feel them.

ⓐ Rudnavovo nám

Kostol a kláštor františkánov (Franciscan Church and Monastery)

The Franciscan church and monastery is a fabulous Gothic building completed in 1297, making it the oldest church in the city. It was also the final stop on the coronation route from the castle. Political shenanigans have been held here over the centuries.

ⓐ Františkánske nám

Kostol a kláštor klarisiek (Church and Cloister of St Clare)

The church and cloister of St Clare was built in the 13th century as a Cistercian nunnery and remains one of Bratislava's most impressive Gothic structures. Today it is a concert venue.

ⓐ Klariská ul

Michalská brána (St Michael's Gate)

St Michael's is the only surviving gate from the medieval fortification of the city. The 51-m (167-ft) tower holds the fascinating Museum of Arms and City Fortifications on six floors and affords a magnificent view from the top.

ⓐ Michalská 24 ⓣ 02 5443 3044 ⓛ 10.00–17.00 Mon–Fri, 11.00–18.00 Sat & Sun, May–Sept; 09.30–16.30 daily, Oct–Apr. Admission charge

Mirbachov palác (Mirbach Palace)

Mirbach is a beautiful rococo palace built between 1768 and 1770 and today is home to the City Gallery of Bratislava, with temporary and permanent exhibits of mostly baroque artists.

ⓐ Františkánske nám 11 ⓣ 02 5443 1556 ⓦ www.gmb.sk
ⓛ 11.00–18.00. Admission charge

○ *The view from Michalská brána (St Michael's Gate)*

Pálffy palác (Pálffy Palace)

Pálffy Palace was discovered to have a Gothic origin during reconstruction, and Celtic and Roman finds were also uncovered. The City Gallery of Bratislava holds temporary and permanent exhibits. A plaque on the wall in the part that is now the Austrian Embassy commemorates Mozart's concert in 1762 at the age of six.

🅐 Panská 19 🕿 02 5443 3627 🌐 www.gmb.sk 🕒 11.00–18.00. Admission charge

Primaciálny palác (Primate's Palace)

The pink neoclassical Primate's Palace was built between 1778 and 1781, and holds some of the world's most precious tapestries (made by royal decree in England for Charles I in the 17th century), which depict the doomed love of Hero and Leander. The building is also famous for a 150-kg (330-lb) iron cardinal's hat atop its pediment and, in 1805 following the Battle of Austerlitz, the Peace of Pressburg was signed here between France and Austria. The pediment is decorated with a mosaic comprising 3,200 coloured pebbles from the Danube. The

CORONATION PATH

The golden crowns in the streets identify the route that was followed by the coronation procession. The route starts at St Martin's and continues along Kapitulská, Prepoštská, Ventúrska and Sedlárska streets to Hlavné námestie. City representatives greeted the king in front of the Old Town Hall, and he then continued to Františkánske námestie.

interior courtyard sports a statue of St George (Slovakia's patron saint) slaying his dragon.

ⓐ Primaciálne nám 1 ☏ 02 5935 6394 ⓦ www.gmb.sk
🕒 10.00–17.00. Admission charge

Stará radnica (Old Town Hall)

Bratislava's Old Town Hall stands testament to its age with three architectural styles incorporated over five centuries. Gothic benches from the 14th century sit next to the 15th-century house and tower built by the first mayor, Jakub, who donated the house to the city when he was elected for the first (of 35) times. The courtyard hosts free concerts over the summer and is home to a lovely café (🕒 09.00–22.00).

The fabulous Museum of Feudal Justice is the oldest in the city and dates back to 1868; it features archaeological objects from the Stone Age to the 1950s, via pots, coins, jewels, swords, paintings and so on. The stairs are steep and spiral, the torture pits and instruments are in the basement, and the retro-manic exhibit on Slovak life in the mid-20th century is rad.

ⓐ Radničná 1 ☏ 02 5920 5130 ⓦ www.muzeum.bratislava.sk
🕒 10.00–17.00 Mon–Fri, 11.00–18.00 Sat & Sun. Admission charge

CULTURE

Slovenská filharmónia (Slovakian Philharmonic)

The beautiful Philharmonic building has rented out part of its premises to Reduta restaurant and casino, but musical performances occur here regularly.

@ Palackého 2 (the box office is in the Reduta building)
① 02 5920 8233 ⓦ www.filharm.sk ⓛ 13.00–19.00 Mon, Tues,
Thur & Fri, 08.00–14.00 Wed

Slovenské národné divadlo (Slovak National Theatre)

The Slovak National Theatre, home to Bratislava's opera and
ballet performances, was built in 1886 to designs by the
alliterative architects Ferdinand Fellner and Herman Helmer.
The fountain, depicting Zeus as an eagle carrying Ganymede
off to be the gods' cup bearer, is the work of Viktor Tilgner
and was placed here in 1888. Inside is no less spectacular with
more than 2,000 lights illuminating its renowned
performances.
@ Hviezdoslavovo nám ⓦ www.snd.sk
Tickets can be obtained from the box office @ Komenského nám
① 02 5443 3890 ⓦ www.ticketportal.sk ⓛ 12.00–17.30 Mon–Fri

Zichyho palác (Zichyho Palace)

Lovely courtyard and house used as a concert venue and gallery.
@ Ventúrska 9 ① 0903 468 776 ⓛ 12.00–18.00, closed Sun

❶ All of Bratislava's museums are closed on Mondays unless
mentioned otherwise.

RETAIL THERAPY

Folk Art Traditional wooden and ceramics plus clothing and
toys. @ Panská 2 ① 02 5443 4874 ⓛ 10.00–18.00 Mon–Fri,
09.00–13.00 Sat, closed Sun

Stará Tržnica An old covered market selling fruit and veg, and with some exceedingly cheap lunch options. ⓐ Nám SNP 25 ⓛ 06.00–24.00

Vinotéka Sv Urbana Local wines at very competitive prices. ⓐ Klobučnícka 4 ⓣ 02 5443 2537 ⓦ www.vinotekasvurbana.sk

TAKING A BREAK

Čajovňa Pohoda £ ❶ Take it easy and get healthy in this Zen tea room decked out with cool tables, mosaics and chess, dominoes, etc. ⓐ Radnicná 1 ⓣ 0905 614 177 ⓛ 09.00–22.00 Mon–Fri, 10.00–22.00 Sat & Sun

London Café £ ❷ Delicious cheap eats, English papers and magazines plus free internet in the courtyard of the British Council. Oh, and strictly no smoking. ⓐ Panská 17 ⓛ 09.00–20.00 Mon–Fri, 09.00–15.00 Sat

Schokocafe Maximilian £ ❸ In the supposedly haunted House of the Black Lady, savour the aroma and taste of all things chocolate, including a fountain. But no smoking, please. ⓐ Hlavné nám 3 ⓛ 09.00–22.00

Verne Café £ ❹ A good mix of locals and expats in this arty den of a café, which serves up booze, coffee, food and atmosphere to the sound of chill tunes. ⓐ Hviezdoslavovo nám 18 ⓣ 02 5443 0514 ⓛ 08.30–24.00 Mon–Thur, 08.30–01.00 Fri, 10.00–24.00 Sat, 11.00–24.00 Sun

AFTER DARK

Restaurants

Pizza Mizza £ ❺ In the Old Town but with a distinctly neighbourhood feel and great oven-cooked pizza. ⓐ Tobrucká 5 ❶ 02 5296 5034 Ⓦ www.pizzamizza.sk 🕒 10.00–23.00 Mon–Fri, 11.00–23.00 Sat & Sun

Botel Gracia ££ ❻ Fabulous views from this floating hotel restaurant and terrace served with good international and grill dishes. ⓐ Rázusovo nábr ❶ 02 5443 2132 Ⓦ www.botel-gracia.sk 🕒 11.00–22.00

Prašná Bašta ££ ❼ Famous cellar space with garden serving huge portions of local cuisine, accompanied by traditional live music. ⓐ Zámočnícka 11 ❶ 02 5443 4957 Ⓦ www.prasnabasta.sk 🕒 11.00–23.00

Reštaurácia Reduta ££ ❽ Fabulous dining under the vaulted ceilings of the Philharmonic building. ⓐ Medená 3 ❶ 02 5443 5242 Ⓦ www.reduta.sk 🕒 11.00–24.00

Camouflage £££ ❾ Cool design and fabulous food in Erdödy Palace (plus adjacent café, Flowers restaurant and club). ⓐ Venturská 1 ❶ 02 5922 7111 Ⓦ www.camouflage.sk 🕒 11.30–01.00

Kogo £££ ❿ Superb Italian, originally from Prague, export their cuisine and relaxed atmosphere. ⓐ Hviezdoslavovo nám 21 ❶ 0902 093 540 Ⓦ www.kogo.sk 🕒 11.00–01.00

Malecón £££ ⓫ The glitterati flock here for the impressive interior, cuisine, superbly mixed cocktails and to mix with other folk whose chauffeurs are waiting outside. ⓐ Nám Ľudovíta Štúra ⓣ 0910 274 583 ⓦ www.malecon.sk ⓒ 11.00–03.00

Mezzo Mezzo £££ ⓬ The late kitchen draws the post-theatre crowd to savour international cuisine with an Asian bent. ⓐ Rybárska brána 9 ⓣ 02 5443 4393 ⓦ www.mezzo.sk ⓒ 08.00–01.00 Mon–Fri, 09.00–01.00 Sat & Sun

◔ *The quirky statue of Ignac Lamar*

Paparazzi £££ ⑬ Sophisticated space with quality Italian cuisine, fine wines and cosmopolitan atmosphere in its dark, warm wood interior divided well for privacy. ⓐ Laurínska 1 ⓣ 02 5464 7971 ⓦ www.paparazzi.sk ⓛ 10.00–01.00

Tempus Fugit £££ ⑭ A classy restaurant in a beautifully restored 15th-century building with covered courtyard and romantic balconies. ⓐ Sedlárska 5 ⓣ 02 5441 4357 ⓦ www.tempusfugit.sk ⓛ 10.00–01.00

Tokyo £££ ⑮ Unremarkable ambience in this restaurant but the courtyard terrace, succulent sushi and spicy Thai make it worthwhile. ⓐ Panská 27 ⓣ 02 5443 4982 ⓛ 11.00–24.00

Bars

17's Bar £ ⑯ A somewhat seedy bar well loved for its simple food, good beer (e.g. Hoegaarden) and ambience. ⓐ Hviezdoslavovo nám 17 ⓣ 02 5443 5135 ⓦ www.17bar.sk ⓛ 11.00–01.00 Mon–Thur, 11.00–02.00 Fri, 13.00–02.00 Sat, 13.00–24.00 Sun

Prazdroj £ ⑰ A Czech pub, with copper fermentation vats, serving Czech favourites Plzeňský Prazdroj (that's Pilsner Urquell) and Kozel along with the hearty food to sop up the brew. ⓐ Mostová 8 ⓣ 02 5441 1108 ⓛ 10.00–02.00

Slang Pub £ ⑱ A drinking den that manages to attract locals and tourists alike for great food and ambience around its

sprawling rooms and long bar. ⓐ Hviezdoslavovo nám 23
ⓣ 02 5443 5073 ⓦ www.slangpub.host.sk ⓛ 10.00–02.00
Mon–Sat, 10.00–01.00 Sun

Café de Zwaan ££ ⓳ Belgium in Bratislava with 13 beers,
including Leffe and Hoegaarden on tap, plus bowls of steaming
mussels all served by efficient and friendly staff. What more do
you want? ⓐ Panská 7 ⓣ 02 5441 9166 ⓦ www.dezwaan.sk
ⓛ 11.00–01.00

Greenwich ££ ⓴ Cocktails and coffee for a suited and booted
crowd oozing after-work sex appeal till way past the mean time.
ⓐ Zelená 10 ⓣ 02 5443 1852 ⓛ 10.00–01.00 Mon–Thur,
10.00–03.00 Fri & Sat, 10.00–24.00 Sun

Hacienda Mexicana & El Diablo ££ ㉑ The usual cheesy Tex-
Mex décor and cuisine entice a lively, young crowd to eat then
party like there was no mañana. ⓐ Sedlárska 6 ⓣ 0904 556 886
ⓦ www.mexicana.sk ⓛ 11.00–03.00 Mon–Sat, 11.00–01.00 Sun

K Bar ££ ㉒ Sheet music papers the walls and you are the star
in this karaoke bar, when the barman isn't doing his adrenalin-
fuelled cocktail show. ⓐ Zelená 8 ⓣ 0905 263 912 ⓛ 11.00–06.00
Mon–Sat, 12.00–06.00 Sun

The Dubliner ££ ㉓ The Irish pub overseas: full of stag parties,
sports fans and the occasional girl. Unsophisticated fun.
ⓐ Sedlárska 6 ⓣ 02 5441 0706 ⓦ www.irish-pub.sk
ⓛ 11.00–03.00 Mon–Sat, 11.00–01.00 Sun

New Town, Bratislava Castle & the river

Surrounding the Old Town proper are ever greater glories to Bratislava's past – including the royal seat, Bratislava Castle. The streets aren't all as narrow and picturesque as the Old Town, but the cobbled lanes outside the city walls leading to the castle are full of character and hidden gems. Away from the cultural part of town, too, you'll find lovely parks, malls and a more local side of Bratislava nightlife.

SIGHTS & ATTRACTIONS

Bratislavský hrad (Bratislava Castle)

The imposing (although it is also known as 'the upside-down table') Bratislava Castle sits on its fortifications looking down on its city. The Slovakian Parliament is located next door – there is a tunnel leading from Parliament to the castle. Some rooms are used today for official government functions (Putin and Bush met here in 2005) but on the whole, the castle is now a museum (see listings in Culture, page 84). Thespians tread the boards here during the summer Shakespeare festival and concerts take place in the magnificent organ room. There is a separate small museum dedicated to the Art of the Far Past of Slovakia, which for a mere 20 SLK is beautifully lit and laid out.

This strategic site was first settled in the Bronze Age, but it was after the Hungarian defeat at the hands of the Turks in 1526 that their Empire's capital was moved from the now-occupied Buda to Bratislava, or Pressburg as it was called then. In 1563, Maximilian II, son of Ferdinand I, was the first Hungarian monarch to be crowned in St Martin's Cathedral. The castle was rebuilt as the royal residence, the crown jewels were stored in the castle's Crown Tower (a replica is on show today) and Bratislava's importance grew. Empress Maria Theresa decreed the castle her summer residence and had it rebuilt as the residence of her favourite daughter, Maria Kristina. Under Josef II the castle was used as a seminary, and from 1802 was used to house troops. In 1811 the castle burned to the ground and remained ruined until 1953 when restoration works, which are ongoing, began.

The grand view takes in the Communist residential creation Petralžka (the industrial area of the city), and large tracts of Austria and Hungary. The grounds and underground well in the courtyard are free to explore.

Exploring the winding but steep streets (Zámocké or Soferove schody and Beblavého) leading up to the castle is part of the experience, but if you've walked enough, then hop on Bus 203 or 207.

Museum 🕐 10.00–17.00. Admission charge

Grounds 🕐 08.00–21.30 May–Sept; 09.00–18.00 Oct–Apr

Chatama Sofera Mauzóleum (Chatam Sofer Memorial)

The recently created Chatam Sofer Memorial is a moving reminder of Bratislava's Jewish community. In 1806, Chatam Sofer, born Moshe Schreiber in 1762, became Chief Rabbi of Bratislava, where he lived and worked till his death in 1836. The memorial has an underground chamber containing 23 graves (including Chatam Sofer's), plus 41 tombstones that escaped destruction of the Jewish cemetery. The glass represents the gravestones that were destroyed. Call in advance to enter.

● *Bratislavský hrad (Bratislava Castle) dominates the city*

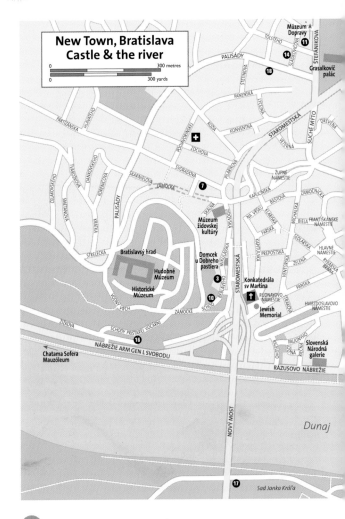

New Town, Bratislava Castle & the river

0 _____ 300 metres

0 _____ 300 yards

TOLSTÉHO

Múzeum Dopravy

ŠTEFÁNIKOVA

SLADKOVIČOVA

Grasalkovič palác

PALISÁDY

ŠTETINOVA

PÁNENSKÁ

LÝCEJNÁ

KOZIA

KONVENTNÁ

STAROMESTSKÁ

PODJAVORINSKEJ

ZOCHOVA

SVORADOVA

DREVENÁ

SUCHÉ MÝTO

VETERNÁ

ŽUPNÉ NÁMESTIE

KAPUCÍNSKA

ZÁMOČNÍCKA

ŠKARNIELOVA

SKALNÁ

NA VŔŠKU

KLARISKA

BASTOVÁ

MICHALSKÁ

FRANTIŠKÁNSKE NÁMESTIE

ZÁMOCKÁ

BIELA

STAROMESTSKÁ

Múzeum židovskej kultúry

PILÁRIKOVA

FARSKÁ

SEDLÁRSKA

PARTIZÁNSKA

SLAVÍNSKÁ

KOZIČKOVÁ

DANOVSKÉHO

MUDROŇOVA

KORENKOVÁ

SMETANOVA

PALISÁDY

RAJTA

Bratislavský hrad

Hudobné Múzeum

Historické Múzeum

VODNÝ VRCH

STRELECKÁ

Domcek u Dobreho pastiera

MIKULÁŠSKA

BEBLAVÉHO

KAPITULSKÁ

PREPOŠTSKÁ

PANSKÁ

VENTÚRSKA

ZELENÁ

HLAVNÉ NÁMESTIE

PREŠOVSKÁ BRÁNA

Konkatedrála sv Martina

RUDNAYOVO NÁMESTIE

STRAKOVA

HVIEZDOSLAVOVO NÁMESTIE

Jewish Memorial

Slovenská Národná galéria

ŽIŽKOVA

SCHODY PRISTAVU VODARNI

SCHODY

ZÁMOCKE

NÁBREŽIE ARM GEN L SVOBODU

PAULÍNYHO

RÁZUSOVO NÁBREŽIE

Chatama Sofera Mauzóleum

RÁZUSOVO NÁBREŽIE

Dunaj

NOVÝ MOST

Sad Janka Kráľa

⊙ Nábr Arm Gen L'Svobodu ☏ 0903 821 432
ⓦ www.chatamsofer.com ⊘ Tram: 4, 12, 17

Domček u Dobreho pastiera (Good Shepherd's House)
This narrow, single-room-span building is a magnificent
example of a rococo *burgher* (citizen) house. Having been built
in 1760, luckily it wasn't destroyed in the 1960s. Narrow, steep
stairs (check out the guy cables keeping house and home
together) lead to three rather shabby floors of exhibits of the
Museum of Historic Clocks – including tools, pictures of clocks,
pictures with working clocks in them and clocks themselves.

⬥ *Domček u Dobreho pastiera is a fine example of rococo architecture*

ⓐ Židovská 1 ⓣ 02 5441 1940 ⓛ 10.00–18.00 May–Sept;
09.30–16.30 Oct–Apr. Admission charge

Grasalkovič palác (Grasalkovič Palace)

Today's Presidential Palace was built as the summer home of
Count Anton Grasalkovič (1695–1771) in 1760 when Maria
Theresa's visits made it the centre of high society. The palace
first became the residence of the President of the Slovak
Republic in the 1940s. The interior includes superb frescoes and
a unique staircase but it isn't open to the public. The manicured
gardens are enjoyed by the public.

ⓐ Hodžovo nám ⓦ www.prezident.sk ⓛ Park: 08.00–22.00
June–Sept; 10.00–20.00 Apr–May; 10.00–19.00 Oct–Mar

Nový most (New Bridge)

The asymmetrical cable-stayed bridge dominates every view of the
city – unless you are on it. The New Bridge was opened in 1972 and
has always been known as the UFO Bridge for its flying saucer-like
restaurant atop its supporting pillars on the Petržalka side. Indeed,
the restaurant is now called UFO. There are 430 steps in the right
leg, but the left leg holds a lift that'll whisk you up to the view of
views. The bridge has lanes for cars, bikes and pedestrians.

ⓣ 02 6252 0300 ⓛ 10.00–22.00. Admission charge, unless you
have a reservation at the restaurant

Sad Janka Kráľa (Jan Kral's Park)

This park, one of the oldest in Europe, was created in 1775 by
Maria Theresa and is named after the Slovak poet Jan Kral. Today
it is not as large as it once was, as the state built the residential

high rise *panelaks* in Petržalka. Restaurant Leberfinger makes a delicious stop in the park and has a terrace, kids' play area and wine cellar.

Restaurant Leberfinger ££ ❸ Plynárenska 7/B ❶ 02 6231 7590 ❹ 11.00–24.00

CULTURE

Historické Múzeum (Museum of History)
Objects illustrate the development of Slovakian society from the Middle Ages to the present day with representative exhibits of furniture, arts, clocks, weapons, ceramics, silver and clothing. The Crown Tower is quite a trek but affords spectacular views.
❸ Bratislavský hrad ❶ 02 5441 1444 ❼ www.snm.sk
❹ 09.00–18.00 May–Sept; 09.00–17.00 Oct–Apr, open Mon. Admission charge for exhibition floors of the castle

Hudobné Múzeum (Museum of Music)
A fine collection of instruments documents Slovakia's rich musical heritage. There is also a recital room with an organ and another annexe in the Luginsland Bastion.
❸ Bratislavský hrad ❶ 02 5441 1444 ❼ www.snm.sk
❹ 09.00–18.00 May–Sept; 09.00–17.00 Oct–Apr, open Mon. Admission charge for exhibition floors of the castle

Múzeum Dopravy (Transport Museum)
The Transport Museum, beautifully housed in Bratislava's first steam railway station, features a selection of carriages, engines, vehicles, equipment and more.

ⓐ Šancova 1/A ☎ 02 5244 4136 ⓦ www.muzeumdopravy.com
🕐 10.00–17.00 May–Sept; 10.00–16.00 Tues–Fri, 10.00–17.00 Sat
& Sun, Oct–Apr Ⓝ Tram: 1, 2, 3, 8; Bus: 210

Múzeum židovskej kultúry (Museum of Jewish Culture)

The Museum of Jewish Culture exhibits a moving collection of
artistic, religious and domestic objects from all over the country.
It also documents the Holocaust and demolition of Bratislava's
Jewish quarter in the 1960s.
ⓐ Židovská 17 ☎ 02 5441 8507 ⓦ www.snm.sk 🕐 11.00–17.00,
closed Sat. Admission charge

Prírodovedné múzeum (Natural History Museum)

The fascinating Natural History Museum holds some 2.4 million
objects. Get your rocks off on four floors of permanent and
temporary exhibitions.
ⓐ Vajanského nábr 2 ☎ 02 5934 9122 ⓦ www.snm.sk
🕐 09.00–18.00. Admission charge

Slovenská Národná galerie (Slovak National Gallery)

The National Gallery has two entrances and two distinct
buildings. The excellent well-lit new wing for temporary
exhibitions has a small entrance on Mostová. A walkway links it
with the Water Barracks, behind the brutal riverside façade,
which holds the permanent exhibitions.
ⓐ Rázusovo nábr 2 ☎ 02 5443 2081 ⓦ www.sng.sk 🕐 10.00–17.30.
Admission charge
ⓘ All of Bratislava's museums are closed on Mondays unless
mentioned otherwise.

RETAIL THERAPY

Aupark The largest mall and entertainment complex in Bratislava so far including cinema, Aquapark, bowling, a casino, and ... Scottish pub. @ Einsteinova 18 ❶ 02 6826 6111 ⓦ www.aupark.sk ⓝ Bus: 50

Polus Bratislava's first mall with shops, entertainment, food and a cinema @ Vajnorská 100 ❶ 02 4444 1234 ⓦ www.poluscitycenter.sk ❸ 07.00–22.30 Mon–Sat, 08.00–22.30 Sun ⓝ Tram: 2, 4, 6; Bus: 50, 51, 198

ÚĽUV Financed by the Ministry of Culture and involved in the design, development and production of Slovak art and craft. Workshops on site. @ Obchodná 64 ❶ 02 5273 1351 ⓦ www.uluv.sk ❸ 10.00–18.00 Mon–Fri, 10.00–14.00 Sat, closed Sun ⓝ Tram: 1, 5, 6, 7, 9

TAKING A BREAK

Bagel & Coffee Story £ ❶ Good breakfast bagels, cakes, wraps, juice and fair trade coffee. @ Štúrova 13 ❶ 02 5263 1656 ⓦ www.bagelcoffeestory.com ❸ 07.00–20.00 Mon–Fri, 10.00–20.00 Sat & Sun ⓝ Tram: 1, 11, 12, 14

Film Café £ ❷ Chilled-out first-floor café with good drinks and food but poor choice of beer, Černá Hora. @ Obchodná 53 ❶ 02 5293 2756 ❸ 10.00–14.00 Mon–Sat, 12.00–14.00 Sun ⓝ Tram: 1, 5, 6, 7, 9

U Čerta £ ❸ Devilish art and ambience in this boozy, friendly, full of old furniture spot. Bar food, armchairs and chess to make you feel right at home. ⓐ Beblavého 2 ⓛ 13.00–24.00 Mon–Fri, 14.00–24.00 Sat & Sun

Dobrá Čajovňa ££ ❹ Grab a spot to recline and infuse the afternoon away. ⓐ Kollárovo nám 16 ⓦ www.dobracajovna.szm.sk ⓛ 12.00–22.00 Mon–Fri, 16.00–22.00 Sat & Sun

Steam & Coffee ££ ❺ This chain provides well-priced healthy food and delicious coffee and teas. Classic. ⓐ Miletičova 23 ⓣ 02 5542 2490 ⓦ www.steamcoffee.sk ⓛ 11.00–24.00 ⓝ Tram: 8, 9, 14

AFTER DARK

Restaurants

Govinda £ ❻ Delicious, cheap curries and sweets from the quietly efficient Hare Krishnas. ⓐ Obchodná 30 ⓣ 02 5296 2366 ⓦ www.iskcon.sk ⓛ 11.00–20.30 Mon–Fri, 11.30–19.30 Sat, closed Sun ⓝ Tram: 1, 5, 6, 7, 9

Chez David ££ ❼ Jewish meals but not a kosher kitchen in this popular eatery with excellent selection of Slovak and Jewish wines. ⓐ Zámocká 13 ⓣ 02 5441 3824 ⓦ www.chezdavid.sk ⓝ Tram: 1, 5, 6, 7, 9

Film Restaurant ££ ❽ Popular Italian restaurant attached to the hotel of the same name and theme. Try the cocktail bar next

door. ⓐ Vysoká 27 ⓣ 02 5293 2794 ⓦ www.filmhotel.sk
ⓛ 11.00–23.00 ⓝ Tram: 1, 5, 6, 7, 9

Kikaku ££ ❾   Recommended sushi spot with only seafood and
veg offerings. Discount available between 15.00–18.00
ⓐ Gorkého 6 ⓣ 02 5443 4783 ⓦ www.kikaku.sk ⓛ 11.30–23.30
Mon–Fri, 18.00–23.30 Sat & Sun

Modrá hviezda ££ ❿   Beautiful 18th-century building with
nook and cranny dining and traditional regional cuisine that
inspires oohs and aahs. ⓐ Beblavého 14 ⓣ 02 5443 2747
ⓦ www.modrahviezda.sk ⓛ 11.00–24.00

Restaurant Matyšak ££ ⓫   Superb. Impeccable service. More
than 4,000 bottles of wine in the cellar plus traditional Slovak
musical accompaniment. ⓐ Pražská 15 ⓣ 02 2063 4053
ⓦ www.hotelmatysak.sk ⓝ Bus: 204, 206, 209, 212

Santé ££ ⓬   Friendly if a little sterile neighbourhood bistro
and restaurant that delivers excellent thin crust pizzas and
bowls of delicious pasta plus breakfast and enchiladas.
ⓐ Dunajská 34 ⓦ www.santerestaurant.sk ⓛ 08.00–23.00
ⓝ Bus: 202, 205

Trafena Husa ££ ⓭   The sophisticated Czech pub chain (from
Prague brewery Staropramen) comes to Bratislava. Hearty
dishes washed down with a large selection of beer.
ⓐ Šafarikovo nám 7 ⓣ 02 5292 5437 ⓛ 07.00–24.00 Mon–Fri,
10.00–24.00 Sat & Sun

Traja mušketieri ££ ⑭ Ritzy cellar with costumed waiting staff serving delicious period dishes (d'Artagnan's Sword) to a happy crowd of wealthy locals, expats and tourists. ⓐ Sládkovičova 7 ⓦ www.trajamusketieri.sk ⓛ 11.00–23.00

Vega Destination ££ ⑮ Travel through space and time in this delicious though not wholly vegetarian hotspot in a futuristic boat building. No smoking. ⓐ Malý trh 2/A ⓦ www.vegadestination.sk ⓛ 11.00–23.00 Mon–Sat, 12.00–18.00 Sun

Caribic's £££ ⑯ This venue is rightly renowned for its seafood. Look for the dolphin mural and lovely winter garden. ⓐ Žižkova 1/A ⓣ 02 5441 8334 ⓦ www.caribics.sk ⓛ 11.00–24.00 ⓝ Tram: 1, 4, 5, 9, 12

UFO £££ ⑰ This iconic place has somewhat painted plate (great presentation, little substance) Mediterranean/Asian cuisine, but good cocktails and the view cannot be beaten. ⓐ Nový most ⓣ 02 6252 0300 ⓦ www.u-f-o.sk ⓛ 10.00–23.00. Club: ⓛ 23.00–04.00 Sat only

U Mamičky £££ ⑱ Gorgeous garden with grill makes a delightful summer place, but superb seafood and homemade flat bread make this home any day. ⓐ Palisady 40 ⓣ 02 5443 4618 ⓛ 11.30–23.00 ⓝ Bus: 203, 207, 208

Bars

Maňana £ A local laid back favourite where you might never see tomorrow on a good night. Kollárovo nám. 15 0905 602 242 www.mananaclub.sk 17.00–05.00. Admission charge for DJ nights

Plzenská £ Superb Czech pub food and beers from this traditional cellar bar named after Plzen, the town in which Pilsner Urquell was invented. Rajská 5 02 5292 0610 10.00–02.00 Mon–Sat, 10.00–24.00 Sun Tram: 4, 6, 7, 11, 14

Radost Chill Out £ Small bar with DJs and friendly folk. Arab cuisine and sheesha fuel the atmosphere. Obchodná 48 0907 723 678 17.00–02.00, closed Sun Tram: 1, 5, 6, 7, 9

Slovak Pub £ A huge pub that manages to be tourist trap *and* local hangout. History, food and beer in raucous surroundings. Reservations recommended. Obchodná 62 02 5292 6367 www.slovakpub.sk 10.00–24.00 Mon–Thur, 10.00–02.00 Fri & Sat, 12.00–24.00 Sun Tram: 1, 5, 6, 7, 9

Hysteria Pub ££ Join the Slovak crowd, Mexican food, disco on Fri & Sat. Odbojárov 9 0910 447 744 www.pub.sk 09.00–01.00 Mon–Fri, 11.00–05.00 Sat, 11.00–24.00 Sun Tram: 2, 4, 6

Obchodná is full of bars and cafes that space doesn't allow us to list. Try the local hangouts of Eden Pub (which never seems to close) and Cestum opposite.

Live music

Hostinec Umelka The pub with a massive beer garden, kilos of grilled meat and some of the best worst live music in the city ⓐ Dostojevského rad 2 ❶ 02 5263 4754 ⓒ 10.00–24.00 Mon–Sat, 11.00–24.00 Sun

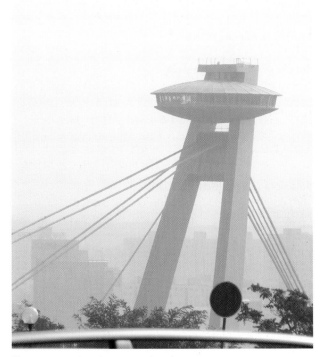

🔺 *Nový most with its famous UFO-shaped restaurant*

Devín Castle & Greater Bratislava

Although a trip to Devín is a must, the other attractions available further out of the city will probably only be seen by those with some time on their hands. These off-the-beaten-path attractions underline all that the city is unknown for. Discover the hidden Bratislava outside the historical centre.

SIGHTS & ATTRACTIONS

Bobová Dráha (Bobsleigh track)

Fantastic fun with the frisson of speed and some danger, the bobsleigh track using carts on wheels. A ski lift services the slope in winter. ☎ 02 5477 1025 ⓦ www.consultingbk.sk/bobo ⏱ 14.00–18.00 Mon–Fri, 10.00–18.00 Sat & Sun. Minimum of five people

Botanická zahráda (Botanical Gardens)

The Botanical Gardens and *skleníky* (greenhouse), part of the Univerzita Komenského, are cheap and delightful. The greenhouse holds various tropical and desert species, while the gardens are a fiesta of native and exotic plants. There's also a Japanese Garden.

ⓐ Botanická ⏱ 09.00–18.00, Apr–Oct; *Skleníky* 09.00–15.00 Mon–Fri, Apr–Oct ⓣ Tram: 1, 5, 9; turn left over the footbridge

Bratislava Zoo & DinoPark

Set in 96 hectares (237 acres) of Carpathian farmland, the zoo, with more than 1,396 animals from 174 species is more than just a viewing platform. The Rehabilitation Station rescues injured and ailing animals from the wild and an education centre proves it's never too early to instil a sense of responsibility for animals and the environment we must all share. The DinoPark, an exposition of scale replicas of various dinosaur genera, is unique to Central Europe and fascinating for kids of all ages. (The word 'dinosaur' is from the Greek *deinos*, meaning terrifying, and *sauros*, meaning 'lizard'.)

ⓐ Mlynská dolina ⓣ 02 6542 2848 ⓦ www.zoobratislava.sk ⓛ 09.00–18.00 Apr–Oct; 10.00–15.00 Nov–Mar ⓝ Bus: 30, 31, 32, 37, 39, 92. Admission charge

Devín Castle

Devín Castle is the historical and cultural heart of the Slovak nation. It is a history lesson in itself, dating back to 5000 BC and

🔺 *Devín Castle is central to the Slovak story*

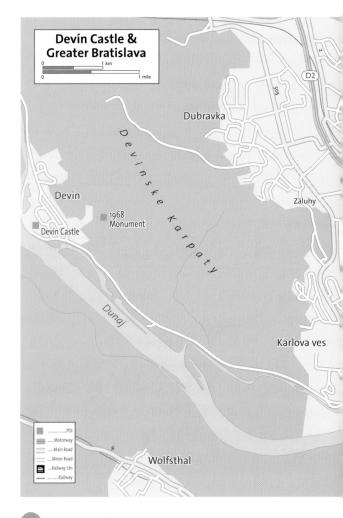

Devín Castle & Greater Bratislava

0   1 km
0   1 mile

Dubravka

Devínske Karpaty

Devín

Záluhy

Devín Castle

1968 Monument

Dunaj

Karlova ves

..........POI
......Motorway
.....Main Road
.....Minor Road
......Railway Stn
.........Railway

9

Wolfsthal

D2

505

94

Podháj

Malokarpatské

Lanovka

Železná
studnička

Lamač

Rázsochy

TV Tower

Lanoland

Kamzík
439

Bobová
Dráha

Briežky

Mestské lesy
v Bratislave

Koliba

Červený most

Vtáčnik

Kútiky

Vinohrady

Bratislava Zoo
& DinoPark

Bratislava-
Hlavná

Slavín
Monument

Staré mesto

BRATISLAVA

505

Botanická
záhrada

D2

Roman Bratislava &
Danubiana Meulensteen
Art Museum

Dunaj

continuing via the Celts, Romans and Hungarians to Napoleon, who – in typical fashion – blew it up in 1809.

The path to the castle is steep and there are many steps, but the history, museums and views are stupendous. Devín sits on a 212-m (695-ft) cliff above the confluence of the Danube and the Moravia rivers, making it the perfect spot for a fortress. After initial settlement in neolithic times, the Celts arrived, followed by the Romans – the Limes Romanus ran along the Danube as the border of the Roman Empire. The slanted building on the way up to the castle holds the remains of the oldest Christian building north of the Danube, the *cella memoriae*, which was unearthed in 1975. It is assumed to be a wooden-roofed Roman chapel, rebuilt many times – indicating extended use. The castle has four gates: Devín Gate, Bratislava and Danube Gates, and Moravia Gate (where the ticket office is now situated). Remains of Slav houses, with their fireplaces in the corner of the house rather than the more usual centre, flank the path, and there are benches to rest and enjoy the view. The facing hillside, Devínska Kobyla, is the edge of the Small Carpathian Mountains and is a protected area for its bio-diversity.

In 863, two Byzantine priests – Cyril and Methodius – were sent by their Emperor, Michael III, to convert the barbarian hordes of Greater Moravia and by doing so broke the Slav nation from German dominance and language. It is thought that Cyril and Methodius established a school in the castle to teach the Slav alphabet they devised. Another reason for Devín's national importance is due to Ľudovít Štúr, who led a quest for Slovak national statehood and created the Slav language standard. There is a plaque commemorating him and the meeting that took place here on 24 April 1836. A nearby exhibition space shows archaeological, cultural and historical finds from the castle grounds over the (numerous) years.

Štúr's quest was not successful at that time, and at the end of the 19th century a column was erected in the castle to honour The Hungarian Soldier, anathema to the Slovaks in this hallowed place of Slav national identity. In 1921 the column was bombed. The only remaining evidence that it stood is a photo in the museum in the upper massif section of the castle.

Devín Castle has three sections: the lower Gothic section built and inhabited by the Gara family; the middle section, with the well and Roman foundations built by the Bartok family in the Renaissance style; and the upper massif section once surrounded by a moat built by the baroque-era Pálffy family. The museum in the massif depicts the changes undergone at Devín under these families, to whom the castle was leased by the ruling dukes of the day.

From the highest point of the massif, popular today for weddings, one can see the natural protection afforded the site with two rivers and the cliff leaving only one side to be fortified. A pictorial plaque shows Devín's place on this strategic junction relative to other castles in the vicinity. Looking down to the smaller Moravia River, the white stone **1968 Monument** is dedicated to those who attempted to swim the Danube to the west and freedom from communism (but were shot or drowned). The Iron Curtain Greenway and Moravia River Flood Plain Greenway provide lovely walking or biking paths. Bratislava is just 9 km (6 miles) away and visiting Devín makes a lovely day out on bikes.

The parking area has basic restaurants and beer gardens for the weary castle visitor and there's another outlet in the castle grounds too.

🕙 10.00–17.00 Mon–Fri, 10.00–19.00 Sat & Sun, May–Sept; 10.00–17.00 Tues–Sun, Apr, Oct–Nov; closed Dec–Mar Ⓝ Bus: 29. Admission charge

Lanoland

Conquer your fear of heights and add to your self-confidence with this superb ropes course. With harnesses and instructors, it's safe and available for kids too. 📞 0918 649 968 🌐 www.lanoland.sk 🕙 15.00–18.30 Tues–Fri, 10.00–18.30 Sat & Sun, closed Mon. Admission charge

Lanovka

The ski lift trundles up and down the slope to Kamzík, running each hour on the hour.

🕙 10.00–18.00 May–Sept. Admission charge (under 5s free).

Mestské lesy v Bratislave (Small Carpathian Mountains), Koliba & Kamzík

The Small Carpathian Mountains drift down almost into Bratislava itself, and provide a respite from Slovakia's capital's increasingly urban lifestyle with walking, biking, hiking and ski trails. This Mestské lesy v Bratislave (Bratislava City Forest) is pinpointed by Kamzík, the TV Tower at Koliba, which was built in 1975 and towers 200 m (656 ft) above ground level. It reaches the dizzy heights of 638 m (2,093 ft) above sea level, however, allowing visitors a superb view of Austria, Hungary and the Czech Republic.

The city forest is a draw to outdoorsy people all year round as it is home to some easy ski slopes with a chair lift and ski pulls as well. The bobsleigh track and high ropes that cross at the summit provide entertainment for all the family, and a trail has been created from Červený most (Red Bridge) to Kamzík along lovely paths and past bubbling brooks and lakes, which become ice hockey practice paradise in winter.

Getting to Kamzík takes some dedication – unless you go by car or taxi, in which case it's simple but you haven't enjoyed the great outdoors. A good round trip is to take Bus 204 or 207 to the last stop, then traverse the E65 highway via the underpass to Patrónka bus stop, take Bus 43 and hop off at any stop once you are in the forest. You will see the City Forest maps and legends at various points along the trail here, which basically follows the road. Walk the trail or hop off the bus at Lanovka in

🔺 *The village of Devín spied from the castle massif*

the Železná studnička area, where the ski lift ascends to the summit of Kamzík. You can walk the trails, too, if you are feeling fit. There are numerous campfire sites, gazebos, BBQ grills, picnic tables and kids' playgrounds along the way.

Once at the summit, explore the various sights and activities, have dinner at one of the restaurants, or sip a cold beer or hot wine while taking in the view from one of the kiosk-type affairs. Then the easiest way down is to follow the road down the city side of the mountain to Bus 203 (about 20 minutes), which will take you into the city centre.

Náučný chodník

The trail from Červený most (Red Bridge) to Kamzík, or vice versa, with information dotted along the way on flora, fauna, history, ecology, etc. Various walking and biking trails are laid out all over the city forest and they do advise sticking to trails as unexploded ordnance from World War II remains in the area. Follow the rules: don't damage the environment, don't litter and don't inadvertently start a wildland fire. Maps and info can be obtained at tourist information offices in Bratislava (see page 136).
ℹ 02 5478 9035 ⓦ www.ba-lesy.sk

Slavín Monument

Bratislava has two elevated landmarks. The 52-m (171-ft) Slavín Monument, the closer of the two to the city centre, is dedicated to the soldiers of the Red Army who died in the liberation of the Slovak lands in World War II. It was unveiled on 4 April 1960 and depicts a Soviet soldier with flag standing on a Nazi swastika around which lie 278 individual graves, although the remains of 6,850 soldiers were brought here. *Slava* means 'glory', and, despite the later yoke of communism after liberation by Russia's Red Army, this is a sacred place. Bratislavans often walk up here to sit, drink, think and watch their city, but always with respect for these fallen soldiers.

To get here, either walk uphill from Palisady or take Bus 203 to the end of the line (at Búdková by the Zlatý Bažant Grill). Then walk along Stará vinárska to the monument, passing by a superb view of the city and some rather ritzy modern villas, including the US ambassador's residence, nicknamed the Little White House.

CULTURE

Danubiana Meulensteen Art Museum

Some 15 km (9 miles) south of Bratislava is the modern art museum set in beautiful grounds on an island in the mighty Danube. Opened in 2000 and designed by architect Peter Zalman, this unique gallery is shaped like a Roman galley and has some 2,000 sq m (6,550 sq ft) of exhibition space, not including the pieces on show in the extensive grounds. The collection here is continually added to and includes works by Slovak and international artists all with some link with the Meulensteen Foundation. Join the likes of King Juan Carlos of Spain and wander around this massive and welcome newcomer to the art scene. There is a shop and café on the premises.
ⓐ Vodné dielo, Čunovo ⓣ 02 6252 8501 ⓦ www.danubiana.info
🕐 10.00–20.00 May–Sept; 10.00–18.00 Oct–Apr 🚍 Bus: 91, 191 to

Čunovo; the 3-km (2-mile) walk to the museum is signposted.
Admission charge

Roman Bratislava

Oh, how the mighty are fallen. In the Bratislavan suburb of
Rusovce is Antická Gerulata, a museum on the site of one of the
furthest garrisons of the Roman military, in the province of
Panonia, the border of which ran along the single line that was
the Danube, the Limes Romanus and the edge of the empire
itself. Gerulata dates back to the 1st century and excavations

---

THE MOTHER-IN-LAW OF EUROPE: MARIA THERESA (1717–1780)

The above nickname came about after she strategically
married off all her 16 children allowing only herself and
favourite daughter Maria Kristina to marry for love. Late
portraits of Maria Theresa show her continually clad in
black following her husband's death. All her 11 daughters
bore the first name Maria and her youngest daughter was
Maria Antonia, better known under her French name
Marie Antoinette.

Maria Theresa was one of the so-called 'enlightened
despots' and bestowed on Bratislava the great honour of
deciding it would be the summer seat of the royal family.
She also decreed the moat and walls surrounding
Bratislava to be filled in and torn down to make way for a
growing populace, and thus a baroque building boom
flourished.

have revealed it as an important military position at an economically strong settlement. Gerulata is marked on the medieval copy of the 4th-century map the Tabula Peutingeriana. Explore the excavations, burial grounds and skeletal remains. A Roman games festival is held in the summer. ⓐ Gerulatská 69 ⓣ 02 6285 9332 ⓛ 10.00–17.00 May–Oct ⓝ Bus: 91, 191; alternatively, follow the cycle route south along the Danube. Admission charge

ⓘ All of Bratislava's museums are closed on Mondays unless mentioned otherwise.

RETAIL THERAPY

Avion Shopping Park Mall life has impacted here – check out Ikea and ice skating. ⓐ Ivanská cesta ⓣ 02 4822 6800 ⓦ www.avion.sk ⓛ 10.00–21.00 ⓝ Bus: 61, 63, 67 plus free shuttle buses from Petržalka

AFTER DARK

Restaurants
Modrý Dom ££ About half an hour from the city centre, this is a lovely village restaurant featuring superb Slovak cuisine (including the autumnal goose feast) and the wines the surrounding area is rightly famous for. For an alternative dessert, grab a cone from one of the best ice cream parlours around. ⓐ Roľnícka 56, Vajnory ⓣ 02 4363 9467 ⓦ www.modrydom.sk ⓝ Bus: 52, 53, 54, 56, 65

Reštaurácia Koliba-Expo ££ ❶ Traditional Slovak hospitality and cuisine in a sublime rural setting. Large terrace and open grill add to the culinary delights. ⓐ Kamzíkov vrch ❶ 02 5477 1764 ⓦ www.koliba-expo.sk

Veža ££ ❷ Enjoy a 360° vista while slowly revolving high atop Kamzík and dining on well-presented dishes. Some tables are static but your fellow diners won't be. ⓐ Cesta na Kamzík 14 ❶ 02 4446 2774 ⓦ www.veza.sk ❶ 11.00–24.00

BARS & CLUBS

Coyote Ugly Taking a lesson from the film, the girls dance on the bar, get the punters well watered and bestow a great evening on a grateful crowd. ⓐ Rožňavská 1 ❶ 02 4463 8923 ⓦ www.kojotky.sk ❶ 11.00–23.00 Mon–Thur, 11.00–04.00 Fri & Sat, closed Sun ⓝ Bus: 53, 63

Harley Davidson Saloon Being on the wrong side of the tracks and by a cemetery hasn't deadened this bikers' club – probably because it's great – grill, terrace and twice nightly strip shows, male and female. ⓐ Rebarborová 1/A ❶ 02 4319 1094 ⓦ www.harley.sk ❶ 11.00–02.00 Sun–Thur, 11.00–06.00 Fri & Sat ⓝ Bus: 208

---

❶ *A swathe of autumn colours cover the foothills of the Small Carpathians*

Malokarpatské (Small Carpathian Mountains)

Heading out of Bratislava on Račianska street, known as Victorious February 1948 street during the communist regime, leads you to the Small Carpathians. This mountain range begins at Devín and, under various names including Slovakia's High Tatras, arches into Ukraine and Romania. The southern slopes are lined with vines.

GETTING THERE

Bratislava's tourist information office (see page 136) organises Wine Route tours to the towns and sights mentioned, making it easy to do in a half day. That said, intrepid folk can drive or take a bus from Bratislava's Autobusova stanica on Mlynské Nivy. The journey to Častá (for Červený kameň) on the bus takes 1 hour 20 minutes, but the bus does stop at all the following places in the Small Carpathians. Bus travellers will need at least two days to see all of the following.

SIGHTS & ATTRACTIONS

Svätý Jur

The picturesque town of St George is just 14 km (9 miles) from Bratislava but retains its village feel. The first written record of St George dates to 1209, although there has been a settlement here since the 4th millennium BC. The town gained full royal privileges in 1615 and reached its golden period when its wines were exported across the region. Original vintners' houses remain around the square, which are characterised by the large central door allowing carriages of grapes to enter the courtyard and production to begin. The town has a number of historical sites: the Gothic 13th-century Church of St George, which holds a white sandstone altar and painting of St George slaying the dragon, plus tombs and sarcophagi. Also, check out the 17th-century wooden bell tower. The ruins of 13th-century Biely Kameň (White Rock Castle) are a 30-minute hike through the forest and are a popular summer destination. There is also a free outdoor pool open in the summer from 08.00–18.00.

Information centre ⓐ Prostredná 64 Ⓦ www.svatyjur.sk

🔺 *The church of St Stephan the King in Modra*

IN VINO VERITAS

The Celts produced wine in this region centuries ago, then better vines arrived with the migration of nations towards the end of the Roman Empire. However, it wasn't until Bratislava became the capital of the Hungarian Empire that the region's wines gained in reputation – after being sipped by the lips of royalty. During communism, quality declined as vineyards were nationalised and only two variations, red and white, were pressed. Nowadays, these wines are once again winning awards. Wines from generations of wine-making families have won the most accolades. Those listed below (and others) provide tours of cellars and samples of wine accompanied by bread, cheese and *oškvarkova masť* (pork dripping).

Hacaj Cajlanská 66, Pezinok 033 640 2696
www.hacaj.sk
Hubert Vinárske 137, Sereď 031 788 1039
www.hubertsekt.sk
Matyšak Holubyho 85, Pezinok 033 640 9023
www.vinomatysak.sk
Mrva u Stanko Orešianska 7/A, Trnava 033 591 4741
www.mrvastanko.sk
Pavelka Cajlanská 126, Pezinok 033 645 1064
www.pavelkavino.sk

September is the month to travel this hilly domain as it is the month of *vinobranie*, the *burčiak* (young wine) festival.

Carnivores must try *husacina* (the accompanying roast goose feast) and *lokše* (potato pancakes). St Martin's Day, 11 November, sees the new wine being blessed and, of course, sampled, and 17–18 November hosts Open Cellar Days where for a small charge you get a map, glass and, best of all, to sample wines from dozens of cellars between Rača and Trnava. A price guide for buying is as follows:

200 SLK for a decent bottle

400 SLK for a sulphur-soaked wine

800 SLK for a (small) bottle of ice wine.

Pezinok

Pezinok is 18 km (11 miles) from Bratislava, is the regional centre and was first mentioned, as Terra Bozen, in written documents in 1208. Originally a mining town, it became a vintner's paradise in the 16th century. In 1647 the town was awarded royal privileges, and the next two centuries saw Pezinok's fame boom due to its superlative wines, industry and railway resulting in a beautiful town with much to see. Pezinok Castle has no museum but does have an excellent restaurant and an exhibit featuring the best 100 Slovak wines – with the possibility to sample and buy.

Information centre ⓐ Radničné nám 9 ⓣ 033 641 2550 ⓦ www.pezinok.sk

Modra

Modra is 25 km (15 miles) from Bratislava and, as with most towns in the region, signs of settlement reach back to around 3000 BC

but remains of a castle in nearby Harmonia and a burial ground to the northeast of the town point to permanent settlements since the 9th century. Modra was conferred the status of Free Royal Town in 1607. Soon afterwards the town built its fortifications with three gateways; some sections plus the Horná brána (Upper Gate) remain. The entire area is crossed by trails for hiking, biking and horse riding, and ski lifts operate all winter.
Information centre ⓐ Štúrova 84 ① 033 647 4302 ⓦ www.modra.sk

Church of St Stephan the King This was initially only the clock tower; the church was added later. ⓐ Corner of Štúrova & Dukelská

Church of Peter & Paul This Lutheran church is located outside the old city walls as law stated that only Catholic churches were allowed inside the city walls. ⓐ Dolná

Červený kameň (Red Rock Castle)

The magnificent Red Rock Castle is the best preserved castle in Slovakia thanks largely to the Pálffy family who lived here from 1583 until 1945, when they abandoned their seat. The castle, so called for the red rock it is built on, rather than of, gradually deteriorated until the 1950s when it was declared a Slovak National Monument and a massive 20-year restoration project began.

Continued warring led to the various Pálffys travelling far overseas, and as was the trend for the period, they brought home spoils of war, art, furniture and medicines. The exhibitions inside the castle, which are only accessible with a tour, show the eclectic and enlightened side of the family.

There is so much to see in this amazing castle. The weird folly room with pebble mosaic floor and waterfalls was used to cool down on hot days. The Turkish curved dagger was used for beheadings with an inner section to slice off ears (Turkish soldiers were paid by the death). Then there's the fireplace and war emblems in the Knights' Room. The cellars, used by the Pálffys for wine, are the largest in Europe.

One of the castle's bastions is open for all to marvel at its sheer size. There are four interior floors with various windows for various weapons to be used in defence, the central support and huge ventilation shafts. Think of all the gunpowder! The extensive grounds can be explored any time and keep an eye out for the albino peacock.

⬥ *The courtyard of Červený kameň*

The castle has no heating, so be prepared if you are visiting in winter. Tours in English are by appointment only, and there is a charge. That said, you can join a Slovak-language tour and use a printed sheet for limited information.

ⓐ Častá, 35 km (22 miles) from Bratislava ❶ 033 690 5803
ⓦ www.snm.sk ⏰ 09.00–17.00 May–Aug; 09.00–16.00 Mar, Apr, Sept & Oct; 09.30–15.30 Nov–Feb, closed 24 & 25 Dec. Admission charge

Astur Falconry ❶ 033 690 5827 ⓦ www.falconry.sk
⏰ 10.00–17.00 1 Apr–31 Oct only; raptor shows at 11.45, 14.15 & 16.15. Admission charge

COAT OF ARMS
The courtyard fountain shows the Pálffy coat of arms – a stag rising from a wheel – which is also the emblem for Bratislava. The story, for the Pálffys anyway, is that one dark and stormy night, when the family were on their way home, a stag leapt out of the forest breaking their carriage wheel and forcing them to remain there that night. As daylight illuminated their predicament, it became apparent that the stag had actually saved their lives as the carriage (purportedly the one on show inside the castle) was on the edge on an abyss. However, despite this stag saving their skins, it appears the Pálffys didn't reciprocate the favour, judging from all the hides and heads hammered to their walls.

Outdoor antique market This takes place on the last Saturday of each month (07.00–12.00), weather permitting. The summer brings horses and ponies to ride plus various historical fencing, jousting and cultural re-enactments. Additionally, night tours show an illuminating side of the castle.

CULTURE

Pezinok
Gallery of Naïve Art Schaubmar Mill was built in 1767 by the Pálffy family. It was then acquired in the 19th century by the Schaubmar family, who kept it working until the early 20th century. The Slovak National Gallery has reconstructed the exterior and renovated the interior, which is a superb and functional technical museum. Sadly, though, the waterwheel is broken. This fine gallery of Slovak and international naïve art was established in 1997. ⓐ Cajlanská 255 ⓣ 033 640 4035 ⓦ www.sng.sk ⓛ 10.00–17.00. Admission charge

Malokarpatské muzeum is located in a vintner's house and tells the history of the town and winemaking – generously doling out samples of the latter. ⓐ MR Štefánika 4 ⓣ 033 641 3347 ⓦ www.muzeumpezinok.sk ⓛ 09.00–12.00 & 13.00–17.00 Tues–Fri, 09.00–15.00 Sat, 13.00–17.00 Sun

The Old Town Hall holds the city museum, a gallery and café. The Marianský stíp column was hidden through communist times and re-erected after the Velvet Revolution. ⓐ Radničné nám ⓣ 033 641 2306 ⓦ www.pezinok.sk

Modra

In the 16th century the Habáni, or Anabaptists, aroused the ire of the Habsburg lawmakers and fled Switzerland. These commune-minded, introverted craftsmen arrived in the area and introduced Modra to their method of ceramic-making. While many potters and painters work at the cooperative in Modra, you can also drop in on one of seven or so independent craftsmen for an unscheduled visit to their workshop. Watch the fluid lines of the objects appear on the potter's wheel. See the changes wrought after kilning and observe the art of detailed freehand painting. Tinkers, master wire craftsmen, can fix cracked and broken pots, dishes and jugs but as people tend to just buy another one nowadays, they have extended their craft into producing intricate art and objects.

Miroslav Malinovský Superb shop and workshop featuring his ceramics plus the works of other artists and kids he teaches. ⓐ Štúrova 60 ⓣ 0903 796 474 ⓛ 09.00–18.00 Mon–Fri, 09.00–12.00 Sat, closed Sun

Slovenská ľudová majolica The ceramics cooperative. Call in advance for a tour. ⓐ Dolná 138 ⓣ 033 647 2941 ⓛ 09.00–15.00

Ľudovít Štúr Museum National leader, linguist and MP who retired, died and is buried here. ⓐ Štúrova 54 ⓣ 033 647 2765 ⓦ www.snm.sk

❶ Remember, all museums are closed on Mondays unless otherwise mentioned.

TAKING A BREAK

Svätý Jur
Rozmarín £ Do drop into the popular and oldest pub in town with beautiful terrace. ❸ Pohradie 56 ❶ 02 4497 1402 ❷ 10.00–22.00 Mon–Thur, 10.00–24.00 Fri & Sat, closed Sun.

Pezinok
Milan Bejdák Vinogallery ££ Superb new cellar for sampling, drinking and eating (but no smoking). ❸ Turecký dom, Radničné nám 1 ❶ 0905 431 329 ❿ www.vinogallery.sk ❷ 16.00–23.00 Thur–Sat

⬤ *A surreal perspective, a Modra ceramics workshop*

Pezinok Castle ££ Try Zámocka in the castle grounds.
ⓐ Mladoboleslavská 5 ⓣ 033 641 2359
ⓦ www.zamockarestauracia.sk ⓛ 11.00–23.00

Radnica ££ Live jazz with your wine. ⓐ Štefánikova 1 ⓣ 033 640
4009 ⓦ www.radnica.com ⓛ 11.00–23.00 Sun–Thur,
10.00–02.00 Fri, 11.00–02.00 Sat

Vinum Galéria Bosen ££ Reservations are a must at the Matyšak
family's hostelry. ⓐ Holubyho 85 ⓣ 033 640 9023
ⓦ www.vinomatysak.sk ⓛ 10.00–23.00

Modra

Vináreň u Ludvika ££ Wine cellar, restaurant and shop in one
beautifully renovated 17th-century wine cellar with terrace, kids'
play area and a wood-fire-heated private dining room.
ⓐ Dukelská 2 ⓣ 0905 970 077 ⓦ www.vinoludvik.sk
ⓛ 11.00–23.00 Mon–Thur, 11.00–24.00 Fri & Sat, closed Sun

U richtára Hacaj ££ Popular and delightful restaurant in a classic
vintner's home stocked with the renowned family wines.
ⓐ Štúrova 93 ⓣ 0903 718 416 ⓛ No fixed hours; call for
information

Červený kameň

The castle The café inside the castle courtyard is open when the
castle is; there is also the Pod Bastou restaurant near the car
park which is open 11.00–23.00.

ACCOMMODATION

Svätý Jur
Horský Hotel Eva £ Situated on the valley floor is this beautiful hotel with rooms, cottage, pub, horse riding, pool and skiing in winter. ⓐ Jozefkovo Údolie ⓣ 02 4497 0507 ⓦ www.horskyhotel-eva.sk

Pezinok
Horský Hotel Istota ££ For a rural stay with a divine wine cellar, try here. It also offers horse riding and skiing. ⓐ Kučišdorfská dolina 27 ⓣ 033 640 0933 ⓦ www.hotelistota.sk

Hotel Vinársky dom ££ This new hotel in the centre of town has various standards of rooms. ⓐ Holubyho 27 ⓣ 033 640 0933 ⓦ www.vinarskydom.sk

Modra
Club MKM ££ Recommended *pension* with more services than you'd expect in Modra and a lovely restaurant. ⓐ Štúrova 25 ⓣ 033 647 2009

Hotel Zochova chata ££ A traditional Slovakian winter and summer resort, this is the hotel for outdoorsy people. An excellent restaurant but little English. ⓐ Piesok ⓣ 033 647 0131 ⓦ www.zochova-chata.com

Červený kameň
Penzión Redrock 55 £ is in the nearby village of Píla.

Further afield

Historically – and culturally – important towns abound. In addition to the following destinations, don't forget that skiing takes place all over Slovakia with good slopes, snow and prices (🅦 www.skislovakia.sk).

GETTING THERE

Trnava

Trnava lies some 40 km (25 miles) from Častá and is located at the end of the Small Carpathian Wine Route. It is a large town and the seat of the Catholic Archbishop. It is just 50 km (31 miles) from Bratislava and easily accessible by bus from the main bus station on Mlynské Nivy.

Around Trnava

Piešťany (85 km/53 miles from Bratislava and 35 km/22 miles from Trnava) has a small airport with connections to Bratislava, along with the more usual bus and train connections.

Nitra

Located 80 km (50 miles) from Bratislava it is well connected by bus from the capital's main bus station on Mlynské Nivy. The bus station in Nitra is about a 15-minute walk from the town centre.

Trenčín

Trenčín, some 100 km (62 miles) from Bratislava, is easily accessible from the city by car, bus and train.

SIGHTS & ATTRACTIONS

Trnava
St Nicolas (Nám sv Mikulaša) and **St John the Baptist**
(Univerzitné nám) are just two of many notable churches.

Západoslovenské múzeum (Western Slovakia Museum) Located
in a 13th-century convent, this museum has cultural and
historical exhibits from the region. ⓐ Muzejné nám 3
🕐 08.00–17.00 Tues–Fri, 11.00–17.00 Sat & Sun

Information centre This is on the ground floor of the
Renaissance Mestká veža (City Tower) on Trojičné nám where
the baroque Holy Trinity statue is located.

🔺 *Trenčín Castle perched above the town*

Around Trnava

Cave formations The karst landscape that exists under much of Slovakia, and particularly around the High Tatras, has created some spectacular cave formations. The closest cave to Bratislava is Jaskyňa Driny (Driny Cave), which has some 410 m (1,345 ft) open to explore, from narrow fissures to medium-size caverns and fabulous sinter deposits. A bus followed by a short walk from Smolenice will take you to the caves. ● 033 558 6200 ● Closed Sun & Nov–Mar. Admission charge

Springs and spas As a result of volcanic activity in the Small Carpathians, there are hidden springs and curative waters bubbling around under the country. One such spa area is Piešťany. This spa resort (on Spa Island, no less) was founded in 1889 and lies in the valley of the Váh River. The water and mud treatments are renowned for their curative effects on arthritis particularly. If you book with a spa hotel, it will arrange transport from the capital. For information and reservations see ● www.spapiestany.com or contact the central booking office ● Winterova 29, Piešťany ● 033 775 7733 ● 07.00–18.00 Mon–Fri

Nitra

The regional centre of Nitra is the oldest city in the country. It is home to the first Christian place of worship in Slovakia (built in 828) and is also where Cyril and Methodius located their school dedicated to the Slav/Slovak alphabet and language after they arrived in the area in 863.

Archaeological remains indicate this area was settled up to 30,000 years ago due to the fertile soil and Nitra is today an economic, cultural and agricultural centre. The tourist information centre will give information, maps and guided tours of the historical centre, which might be the best idea for a short visit here as there is much to see and do. Skiing, hiking and horse riding are popular outdoor pursuits and the good info people will help with these as well.

Nitra, like Rome, was built on seven hills and these make for lovely hikes. If you can only visit one, head for Zobor and follow the hour-long educational trail to the summit. Take Bus 9 to the end stop for the trailhead.

The central historical area is where you will find the Royal Way and the Church of Sts Cyril & Methodius (ⓐ Piaristická).

Nitra Castle This building dominates the landscape. Its cathedral is in the Upper Town, where the Bishop's Palace and the Great and Small Seminaries are located. Here you will also find a lovely city park and the Statue of Corgoň (ⓐ Pribinovo nám), who was supposed to have saved the castle from the Turks and has the locally brewed beer named after him.

Nitra Synagogue The woman's gallery of this former synagogue houses a poignant permanent exhibition of the Holocaust, put together by the Museum of Jewish Culture based in Bratislava. ⓐ Pri synagóge 3 ⓣ 0908 712 882 ⓦ www.slovak-jewish-heritage.org ⓛ 13.00–18.00 Tues, Sat & Sun, 09.00–12.00 & 13.00–18.00 Wed & Thur, closed Mon & Fri. Admission charge

Vasil Tower At the cathedral, ask for the key to this tower to check out the spectacular view of the city and environs.

Tourist information ⓐ Štefánikova 1 ⓣ 037 741 0906
ⓦ www.nitra.sk & www.nisys.sk ⓛ 08.00–18.00 Mon–Fri,
08.00–12.00 Sat, closed Sun

Trenčín

Trenčín is spectacularly pinpointed by its castle, one-time seat of
the excellently named Mighty Lord of the Váh and the Tatras,
Matúš Csák III. While you are there, don't miss the Roman
inscription on the castle walls near the Hotel Tatra dating to the

ⓞ *Church of St Peter Xaverský, Trenčín*

1st century AD, nor the Renaissance parish stairway built in 1568. On a different note entirely, this town is also famous for its fashion designers and for the country's largest music festival at the airport in July.

Bažant Pohoda Festival This attracts big names and thousands of spectators. The airport is almost limitless in capacity. Check for exact dates and line-up. Ⓦ www.pohodafestival.sk

Castle This building remains the centre of things for culture (historical tournaments and festivities in the summer) and history (paintings, weapons and objects in museums in the castle and around town). Ⓦ www.muzeum.sk ⏱ 09.00–17.30 Tues–Sun, May–Aug; 09.00–16.30 Tues–Sun, Sept; 09.00–15.30 Tues–Sun, Oct–Apr

Executioner's House This incongruously picturesque property dates to 1580 and is one of the few medieval burgher houses remaining in Trenčín. ⓐ Matúšova 14. Admission charge

Museums and events Check out this well-resourced website for what's happening where. Ⓦ www.muzeum.sk

Trenčianske Teplice Close by, this can be reached by train and bus from either Bratislava or Trenčín. It has an annual film festival held in June (Ⓦ www.artfilm.sk) featuring films of all genres from all over the world. Another reason to come here is for the thermal waters and their curative properties – a thermal pool and beautiful Moorish *hammam* feature in the spa facilities.

Walking & biking The River Váh and Lesopark Brezina provide ideal walking and bike trails. The excellent tourist information office provides all kinds of info, souvenirs, tickets and a wonderful website ⓐ Sládkovičova ⓣ 032 16186 ⓦ www.trencin.sk ⓛ 08.00–18.00 Mon–Fri, 08.00–16.00 Sat, closed Sun, 15 Apr–14 Oct; 10.00–17.00 Mon–Fri, 10.00–12.00 Sat, closed Sun, 15 Oct–14 Apr

Further information ⓦ www.slktn.sk

AFTER DARK

Nitra
Devil's Pub £ Get up to no good with the locals for a night's drinking, partying or special event. ⓐ Kmeťkova 2 ⓣ 037 772 1392 ⓦ www.devilspub.sk

The Irish Times Pub £ Food, live music, good times and Guinness all served in an authentic pub atmosphere. ⓐ Kupecká 12 ⓣ 037 657 5106 ⓦ www.irishtimespub.sk ⓛ 08.00–01.00 Mon–Thur, 08.00–03.00 Fri & Sat, 11.00–24.00 Sun

Trenčín
Jameson Pub £ Good food, beer and weekend disco. ⓐ Mierové nám 13 ⓣ 0905 255 335 ⓛ 09.00–24.00 Mon–Thur, 09.00–04.00 Fri, 16.00–04.00 Sat, 16.00–24.00 Sun

Korzár £ Excellent food is served in this pub restaurant that delivers on all counts. ⓐ J Braneckého 6 ⓣ 032 649 1755

🕐 10.00–23.00 Mon–Thur, 10.00–01.00 Fri, 10.00–24.00 Sat, 11.00–23.00 Sun

ACCOMMODATION

Trnava
Ubytovňa ŽOS £ Good (but little English spoken) hostel some 20 minutes southeast of town on foot or take Bus 5. ⓐ Koniarekova 21 ⓘ 033 556 7438

Hotel Barbakan ££ Standard rooms and services are made more attractive by a good restaurant and lovely cellar pub with copper brew tanks ⓐ Štefánikova 11 ⓘ 033 551 4022 ⓦ www.barbakan-trnava.sk

Hotel Dream ££ Well located in the historical centre, with comfortable rooms, an excellent cellar restaurant and terrace. ⓐ Kapitulská 12 ⓘ 033 592 4111 ⓦ www.hoteldream.sk

🔺 *Listening to a performance at the annual Trenčianske Teplice art film festival*

Nitra

Hotel Átrium ££ Refurbished hotel in the city centre and with a winter garden restaurant. Internet and mod cons as standard. ⓐ Štefánikova 8 ⓣ 037 652 3790 ⓦ www.hotelatriumnitra.sk

Hotel Zlatý Kľúčik ££ Award winning restaurant, lovely rooms and fitness centre/sauna on Zobor hill. ⓐ Svätourbanská 27 ⓣ 037 655 0205 ⓦ www.zlatyklucik.sk

❶ Trade fairs at the International Exhibition Centre double the price of accommodation, so to save money, make sure your visit doesn't coincide with one of them (ⓦ www.agrokomplex.sk).

Trenčín

Autocamping OSTROV £ Camp on an island surrounded by the Váh. ⓐ Na ostrove ⓣ 032 743 4013

Hotel Brezina ££ Rural retreat for families and businessmen with buffet and outdoor BBQ pits. ⓐ Lesopark Brezina ⓣ 032 652 8171 ⓦ www.hotel-brezina.sk

Hotel Tatra £££ Award-winning hotel and restaurant built by Baron Armin Popper in 1901 and superbly situated beneath the castle. ⓐ Gen M R Stefánika 2 ⓣ 032 650 6111 ⓦ www.hotel-tatra.sk ⓛ Restaurant: 11.30–14.30 & 18.00–22.00

---

❿ *Dragon signs denote pharmacies in the Old Town*

PRACTICAL information

Directory

GETTING THERE

By air

Bratislava is served for national and international flights by MR Stefánik airport, although there aren't any direct scheduled flights from the UK to Bratislava at the time of publication. Budget airlines, including the Slovak low-cost carrier SkyEurope, do fly here direct from many European cities. Flying time from Britain is around 2 hours.

Ryanair ☎ 02 4870 4870 Ⓦ www.ryanair.com

SkyEurope ☎ 02 4850 4850 Ⓦ www.skyeurope.com

Many people are aware that air travel emits CO_2, which contributes to climate change. You may be interested in the possibility of lessening the environmental impact of your flight through the charity Climate Care, which offsets your CO_2 by funding environmental projects around the world. Visit Ⓦ www.climatecare.org

By rail

With its prime location in the centre of Europe, Bratislava is well linked with the rest of the continent by rail and this is how many passengers currently arrive in the country. Slovakia's trains are operated by The Railways of the Slovak Republic (Ⓦ www.zsrtrain.sk) and all international trains arrive at Bratislava Hlavná stanica (central train station). The search function for trains is in Slovak only at Ⓦ www.slovakrail.sk. Try the excellent German Rail site (Ⓦ www.bahn.com) for international timetables and reservations. Alternatively, in the

UK visit Rail Europe (@ 178 Piccadilly, London W1 ☏ 08708 371 371 ⓦ www.raileurope.co.uk). Journey time from the UK is about 24 hours.

Driving from the UK
By road from Calais, head towards Dunkirk and cross the frontier into Belgium. From Belgium, you will journey all the way to Bratislava through the Netherlands, Germany and Austria on the E40. However, the road will have different numbers and letters in the various countries and, while it remains the E40, it may not always be called that.

ENTRY FORMALITIES
Visitors from the UK, Ireland, other EU countries, the USA, Canada, Australia and New Zealand need only a valid passport to enter the Slovak Republic and can stay for up to 90 days, although the entry visa as such is valid for 180 days. Visitors from South Africa must obtain a visa from an embassy or consulate before arriving in the country, and visas vary in cost.

MONEY
The Slovak Republic (Slovenská Republika) issued its currency in 1993 after splitting from the Czechs: the Slovak Korunny (SLK, SKK or crown) is divided into 100 hellers. Notes come in denominations of 20, 50, 100, 200, 500, 1,000 and 5,000 SLK; coins come in 50 hellers and 1, 2, 5 and 10 SLK. Banks are open 09.00–18.00 Mon–Fri and 09.00–12.00 Sat, but *bankomats* (ATMs) are prevalent. Money exchange offices also exist, but

ATMs provide a much better rate of exchange. Do not try to break large notes in small shops or with taxi drivers.

HEALTH, SAFETY & CRIME

The water is safe to drink and there are no health issues for Bratislava. That said, as Slovakia is a landlocked country, you may want to be wary of shellfish. Hospitals are not quite up to British standards for cleanliness or facilities, but for emergencies (the treatment of which is free up to a limit) they are sufficient.

Crime is low on the radar for the average tourist, but be aware of potential pickpockets and cunning muggers in crowded areas. Items left unattended or on display will disappear. The police are armed and visible in green or blue uniforms but are not usually English-speaking.

OPENING HOURS

Shops 09.00–18.00 Mon–Fri
Malls and large shops 09.00–22.00 daily
Post offices 07.00–19.00 Mon–Fri
Banks 09.00–18.00 Mon–Fri, 09.00–12.00 Sat
Offices 09.00–17.00 Mon–Fri
Museums 09.00–18.00, closed Mon
Restaurants The super economical Slovak lunch deal is served from 11.00–15.00, while kitchens usually close at 22.00

TOILETS

Public toilets are around, but you usually have to pay a few crowns for the privilege of them having been cleaned and having toilet paper. Alternatively, pop into a café or restaurant, preferably buying something in return, or use the lobby facilities of one of the larger hotels.

CHILDREN

You might think kids and museums don't go together too well, but many of the exhibits in Bratislava are from its medieval past so weapons and torture instruments may well increase their level of interest. You can tire them out in the great outdoors with summer walks and winter tobogganing (any toy/sport shop sells cheap sledges) or at one of the numerous playgrounds around town.

AquaPark Indoor and outdoor swimming with year round availability. ⓐ Einsteinova 18 ⓣ 02 6820 1031 ⓦ www.aulandia.sk ⓛ 10.00–22.00

Bibiana The International House of Art for Children where your kids can participate in one of the numerous events, workshops and dramas. The nearby graffiti is actually work done by the kids. Open invitation on Sat & Sun; call in advance for weekday activities. ⓐ Panská 41 ⓣ 02 5443 1308 ⓦ www.bibiana.sk ⓛ 10.00–18.00

Dráčik Local children's toy shop with huge selection and toys galore out of their boxes to be test-run. ⓐ Obchodná 2 ⓦ www.dracik.sk ⓛ 10.00–21.00

Slovak National Gallery Call for details on its Kids' Creative Workshops. ⓐ Rázusovo nábr 2 ⓣ 02 5443 2081 ⓦ www.sng.sk ⓛ 10.00–17.30

Bratislava Zoo & DinoPark Fascinating for kids of all ages.
ⓐ Mlynská dolina ① 02 6542 2848 ⓦ www.zoobratislava.sk

COMMUNICATIONS
Phones
Local, national and international calls can be made from call
boxes in the street, in post offices and in some underpasses
using coins or phonecards. Some internet cafés also offer cheap
international calls. Discount calling cards such as Telecard
(ⓦ www.telecard.sk) enable you to call with up to 70 per cent
discount overseas from anywhere in the world. If you are in
Bratislava for any length of time, pick up a local pre-paid SIM card
for your mobile. Local networks: Orange (ⓦ www.orange.sk),
T-Mobile (ⓦ www.t-mobile.sk) and Telefónica O$_2$ Slovakia.

To make an international call dial 00 + the country code +
the phone number, omitting the initial zero. Country codes: UK
44, USA and Canada 1, Australia 61, New Zealand 64, South Africa
27, Ireland 353.

Slovakia's country code is 421. Bratislava's provincial area
code, 02, must be dialled before all phone numbers, even for
local calls. Mobile phone numbers here are easily recognisable
as they all begin with 09.

International information ① 12 149
National information ① 1181.
Yellow Pages ⓦ www.yellowpages.sk

Post
The main post office is at Nám SNP 35 (ⓦ www.slposta.sk
🕒 07.00–20.00 Mon–Fri, 07.00–18.00 Sat, 09.00–14.00 Sun).

A stamp for a postcard/letter less than 20 g costs 21/23 SLK to another EU country and 28/34 SLK to the rest of the world. Postboxes are orange.

Internet
Most hotels now provide at least one free internet-enabled computer in the hotel lobby. If you have your own laptop or handheld device with you, there are numerous Wi-Fi spots in the city such as in Primacialne nám, in front of the Primate's Palace. Internet cafes abound; here are just a couple.
Net Café Pay in advance and sign into your account. ⓐ Vysoká 37 ⓣ 02 5296 2847 ⓒ 08.00–22.00
Kristi@n Internet café, WiFi and good beer too. ⓐ Michalská 10 ⓣ 02 5443 4038 ⓦ www.kristian.sk ⓒ 11.00–24.00

Listings magazines, newspapers and maps
Press International newsagents sell all the major international daily, weekly and monthly titles. Various venues stock magazines such as *City Guide Bratislava*, *Favourite Places* and *Enjoy Bratislava*. There's also an English monthly guide, *What's On Bratislava and Slovakia* (costing 50 SLK) and Slovak-language listings (easy to read nonetheless) *Club agenda* and *Kam do mesta*. The *Slovak Spectator* is the country's only English language newspaper and is printed each Monday (ⓣ 02 5923 3300 ⓦ www.slovakspectator.sk).

For maps and guides, visit the Academia bookstore at ⓐ Štúrova 9 ⓣ 02 5296 8772 ⓒ 08.00–18.30 Mon–Fri, 09.00–12.30 Sat, closed Sun ⓝ Tram: 1, 11, 12, 14

Twin City Journal is an excellent monthly magazine in German, English and Slovakian listing what's on in Bratislava and Vienna. It is available in Bratislava from the tourist information offices listed under Further Information below.

ELECTRICITY
Slovakia's electricity supply is 220 volts. Plugs have two round pins, so UK electrical devices will need an adaptor. Visitors from the USA will also need a transformer.

TRAVELLERS WITH DISABILITIES
Bratislava was not designed to be and has not yet been updated to be accessible to those with disabilities. All public transport needs to be stepped up into, and almost every major attraction and sight has innumerable steps. Presumably, as with other countries new to the EU, this will slowly change. Hotels usually do have rooms suitable for those with special needs. Ironically, persons with disabilities can enter most museums free of charge, but sadly many locations involve climbing up steep stairs ...

FURTHER INFORMATION
The internet is a vital tool for anyone planning a holiday and much information can be gleaned from it before you even step on a plane. Once in Bratislava, contact one of the helpful tourist information offices for information, tours and printed matter.
Main tourist information office @ Klobúčnicka 2 ✆ 02 5443 3715 ⓦ www.bratislava.sk 🕑 08.30–19.00 Mon–Fri, 09.00–19.00 Sat, 08.30–19.00 Sun

You will also find tourist information centres at the following:

Airport ✆ 02 4363 0306 🕙 09.00–23.00 daily, 1 May–14 Oct;
09.00–19.00 Mon–Fri, 09.00–17.00 Sat, 12.00–19.00 Sun,
15 Oct–30 Apr

Passenger port ⓐ Fajnorovo nábr 2 ✆ 02 5274 316 02
🕙 09.00–16.30 Mon–Fri, 09.30–16.30 Sat & Sun, June–Sept

Railway station ✆ 02 5249 5906 🕙 08.00–19.00 Mon–Fri,
09.00–16.00 Sat & Sun

BACKGROUND READING

It's not just historically that the Slovak Republic has played
second fiddle to ruling nations and neighbouring Czechs. In
literature, too, Czech authors remain dominant – but that's not
to say the Slovaks have no voice. For an insight into the Slovak
oral storytelling tradition, look no further than *Slovak Tales for
Young and Old*, a true sum of its parts. Tales were collected and
edited by Pavol Dobsinsky, modernised by Peter Strelinger,
translated by Lucy Bednar and illustrated by Martin Benka, one
of Slovakia's most famous artists. Simple, tasty Slovak food is
beautifully presented in *The Best of Slovak Cooking* by Sylvia
Galova-Lorinc and John & Sylvia Lorinc. Take home dumplings,
stuffed cabbage, and poppy seed and nut rolls. Also read Janko
Kráľ, Ján Kalinčiak and Jozef Cíger-Hronský.

Emergencies

EMERGENCY NUMBERS

There are separate numbers for the police, fire and ambulance services, but the international emergency number **112** will get you through to an operator who will then direct your call to the service you require.

Ambulance 155
City police 159   **Fire and rescue service** 150
State police 158   **Traffic police** 154

MEDICAL EMERGENCIES

Pharmacists are well known for being able to treat common ailments, but the real trick is conveying your problem if it isn't something that can safely be pointed at. *Lekáreň* (pharmacies) have the green cross sign. There is an open-all-hours one at ⓐ Nám SNP 20 ⓣ 02 5443 2952

Emergency medical treatment is available free of charge to British citizens to a certain extent. For repatriation or an air ambulance, for example, you will need to pay or have insurance.

The following are the most central hospitals in the area:
Nemocnica Staré Mesto ⓐ Mickiewiczova 13 ⓣ 02 5729 0111
Nemocnica s poliklinikou ⓐ Ružinovská 6 ⓣ 02 4823 4114
Nemocnica s poliklinikou ⓐ Limbová 5 ⓣ 02 5954 1111

STOLEN & LOST PROPERTY

Your best bet is to report it to a policeman. State policemen wear green uniforms, and drive green and white cars. City policemen are in blue uniforms, drive white cars and have limited powers. The two central police stations are at **Medená 2** and **Obchodná 42**, where you may or may not find someone speaking English.

❶ If you feel a city policeman is ripping you off – there have been tales of illegal on-the-spot fines being imposed – call the state police.

EMBASSIES
Australian and New Zealand visitors are looked after by the British Embassy at ⓐ Panská 14–16 ❶ 02 5998 2000 ⓦ www.britishembassy.sk
Canadian ⓐ Carlton Courtyard and Savoy Buildings, Mostová 2 ❶ 02 5920 4031
Republic of Ireland ⓐ Carlton Courtyard and Savoy Buildings, Mostová 2 ❶ 02 5930 9611
South African Honorary Consulate ⓐ Révova 27 ❶ 02 5441 7841
UK ⓐ Panská 14–16 ❶ 02 5998 2000 ⓦ www.britishembassy.sk
USA ⓐ Hviezdoslavovo nám ❶ 02 5443 0861. Emergency only: 0903 703 666 ⓦ www.usis.sk

EMERGENCY PHRASES
Help! Pomoc! *Pomots!*　　　　**Fire!** Pożar! *Po-jar!*
Stop! Stop! *Stop!*
Call an ambulance/a doctor/the police/the fire service!
Wezwać pogotowie/lekarza/policję/straż pożarną!
Ve-zvach po-go-toh-vyeh/le-ka-jah/po-lee-tsyeh/straj po-jar-nom!

INDEX

The publishers would like to thank the following individuals and organisations for providing their copyright photographs for this book.

Wendy Wrangham: all photos except: City of Bratislava p11, p15, p32, p36; Trenčín Tourist Board p121: the Art Film Festival, p127: Fotolia (Vladimír Radosa).

Copy editor: Sandra Stafford
Proofreader: Ian Faulkner

Send your thoughts to
books@thomascook.com

- Found a great bar, club, shop or must-see sight that we don't feature?

- Like to tip us off about any information that needs updating?

- Want to tell us what you love about this handy little guidebook and more importantly how we can make it even handier?

Then here's your chance to tell all! Send us ideas, discoveries and recommendations today and then look out for your valuable input in the next edition of this title. As an extra 'thank you' from Thomas Cook Publishing, you'll be automatically entered into our exciting prize draw.

Send an email to the above address (stating the book's title) or write to: CitySpots Project Editor, Thomas Cook Publishing, PO Box 227, The Thomas Cook Business Park, Unit 18, Coningsby Road, Peterborough PE3 8SB, UK.